"*Morning Thoughts* provides daily challenges to promote positive thinking and a successful Christian walk. Ideal for use in addition to daily Bible reading, the Scriptures, prayers, and challenges inspired by songs are sure to help readers grow a stronger relationship with Christ."

Jennifer Taylor
Freelance writer
Springfield, MO

"*Morning Thoughts* is a daily devotional unlike any other. It will encourage you to draw near to God and invite His relevance into your life. Each devotion includes Scripture, prayer, or links to song lyrics that will inspire and challenge you."

Rose Brooks, M.Ed., LPCI
The Neurobehavioral Clinic
Nederland, TX

Morning
Thoughts

Morning Thoughts

365 Challenges to Help You Focus on Christ

JOSHUA DOMBROSKY

LUCIDBOOKS

Morning Thoughts

Published by Lucid Books in Brenham, TX.
www.LucidBooks.net

Note: The organizations mentioned and the artists of the songs haven't endorsed the book.

First Printing 2012

ISBN-13: 978-1-935909-46-0
ISBN-10: 1935909460

Contents

About the Book

While working on my Masters, I learned just how important thinking is. I realized my days are better if I start my mornings off with something to think about that helps me focus on Christ. Then I have something life-giving and nurturing to mediate on while I go about my day. This book consists of Scripture and challenges for 329 days; challenges from songs for 24 days; and 12 days of reminders to pray.

I picked the scripture based on topics that I thought most Christians, or people in general, struggle with. Some of the topics include love, anger, sacrifice, friends, our tongue, self-control, faith, and worship. Each scripture has a challenge that goes along with it. Some challenges are to physically do something, while others require self evaluation. Hopefully a few of the challenges will push you to try activities you are not normally comfortable doing. I will be the first to say that I need these challenges as much as anyone else could.

I never have been a music fanatic. Before starting this book, I didn't listen to much radio other than ESPN radio. When I did listen to music, my mind would normally drift off to something else. While working on this book, I began to listen to Christian radio on a consistent basis. I started to focus on the lyrics and thought it would be good to include some songs in the challenges. I knew a few of the songs I wanted to include, but had nowhere near 24 songs. As time passed the list filled out. Each song challenge has its own page on my website. Each page includes one or more of the following: a link to read the lyrics to the song, a link to listen to the song, and a link to watch the songs music video or a performance of the song by the artist. The music to some of these songs may not be your style, but that is not the focus. Focus on the lyrics and how they can relate to your life.

Prayer is one of the topics covered in the challenges as well, but I wanted to include things that could help us remember to pray throughout the day. It is easy to grow busy and neglect prayer, and it helps if we have reminders that encourage us to pray. These are not prayers for you to repeat or anything like that. They are common experiences that we can turn into an opportunity to pray for others.

I believe if any group of people is going to reach their potential, every individual in that group must strive to improve each and every day. I can't say I believe we as Christians in America are doing this. I can't say that I strive for improvement every day. It seems to me that we are far too comfortable. Saying a prayer and going to church is not all that is required. A relationship with Christ is a lifelong journey that requires us to get out of our comfort zones. If you disagree with that, then this isn't the book for you.

Everyday will not be eye opening for you, but I hope and pray that at least one day will help you become more like Christ. Room is provided each day for you to reflect on your day and your challenge. This book is not meant to replace reading the Bible on a daily basis, but to complement it.

More About a Relationship With Christ

"for all have sinned and fall short of the glory of God,"
Romans 3:23

We are all sinners.

"For the wages of sin is death, but the gift of God is eternal life in Christ Jesus our Lord."
Romans 6:23

We all deserve death, or eternal separation from God (separation from God is spent in Hell), because of our Sin. God offers us eternal life through Jesus.

"For God so loved the world that He gave His only begotten Son, that whoever believes in Him should not perish but have everlasting life."
John 3:16

God sent Jesus to die on the cross for our sins so that we can spend eternity with Him.

"But He was wounded for our transgressions, He was bruised for our iniquities; The chastisement for our peace was upon Him, And by His stripes we are healed."
Isaiah 53:5

Jesus was bruised, beaten, and killed for our sins.

"Now on the first day of the week, very early in the morning, they, and certain other women with them, came to the tomb bringing the spices which they had prepared. But they found the stone rolled away from the tomb. Then they went in and did not find the body of the Lord Jesus. And it happened, as they were greatly perplexed about this, that behold, two men stood by them in shining garments. Then, as they were afraid and bowed their faces to the earth, they said to them, Why do you seek the living among the dead? He is not here, but is risen! Remember how He spoke to you when He was still in Galilee, saying, 'The Son of Man must be delivered into the hands of sinful men, and be crucified, and the third day rise again.'"
Luke 24:1-7

Jesus defeated death. He is alive today.

"Jesus said to him, I am the way, the truth, and the life. No one comes to the Father except through Me."
John 14:6

Jesus is the only way to Heaven. Christ tells us that He is the only way to His Father (God), who is in Heaven.

"For by grace you have been saved through faith, and that not of yourselves; it is the gift of God, not of works, lest anyone should boast."
Ephesians 2:8-9

Our salvation is through faith. No amount of good works will get us to Heaven.

"that if you confess with your mouth the Lord Jesus and believe in your heart that God has raised Him from the dead, you will be saved."
Romans 10:9

If you believe that Christ died for your sins and rose again to defeat death, then all you have to do is ask Christ to forgive you for your sins and to be your Savior.

Do you have a personal relationship with Christ? These verses tell us that we are all sinners, that we deserve to spend eternity in Hell apart from God, that Christ died for our sins, that He rose again, that a relationship with Him is the only way to heaven, and that if we want a relationship with Him, then all we have to do is believe and ask. A relationship with Christ does not consist of a one time prayer. If we meet someone once and leave it at that, do we really have a relationship with them? The awesome thing is that if we truly meet Christ once, then we will desire to have a relationship with Him.

Beginning a relationship with Christ is the best thing we can do, but it does not mean our life will be easy from that point on. A relationship with Christ is a lifelong journey. One that will consist of ups and downs. It may cost you some friendships. It may mean changing your lifestyle. It may mean giving up some things you don't want to give up. It will mean messing up each and every day and asking the Lord to help you do better. Do you want a life changing relationship with Christ? A relationship with you is so important to Him that He died for you.

If you realize you are a sinner in need of a Savior, then all you have to do to begin a relationship with Christ is tell Him that you understand that you are a sinner; tell Him you believe that He came to die for your sins; tell Him that you believe He defeated death; ask Him to forgive you for your sins and save you.

If you do this, please let another Christian know.

Example

"A Scripture will appear here unless the day's topic is a song or a reminder to pray."

A daily challenge will appear here.

The row below is to help you keep track of your daily praying/reading and to write what specific aspect of life you are working on (anger, listening, serving...). Strive to improve your areas of weakness.

☐ Pray   ☐ Read   Currently working on _____

The Evening Reflection is a space for you to reflect on how you did with the challenge for that day. Feel free to write about what is going on in your life, prayer requests, or anything else you want to use it for.

Evening Reflection

Day 1

"if My people who are called by My name will humble themselves, and pray and seek My face, and turn from their wicked ways, then I will hear from heaven, and will forgive their sin and heal their land."

2 Chronicles 7:14

Do you think our land needs to be healed? This verse tells us that healing begins with individuals. If we want to see our land change, then we must change. If we want our land to reflect Christ, then we must reflect Christ to our land. We can't continue with the status quo. The status quo is what has brought us to this point. We as Christians are to blame for the direction our country has taken, not our government. We have failed Christ and our country. If you desire to see our land turn back to a land that glorifies God, I challenge you to start with yourself. Pray for God to show you how to become more like Jesus, and start the process today.

☐ Pray   ☐ Read   Currently working on _____

Evening Reflection

Day 2

"For as he thinks in his heart, so is he"

Proverbs 23:7

What does your heart look like? Is it tender, caring, and giving like Christ or is it hard, self-serving, and stingy like the world? Often times we have a negative outlook on life because our heart is not in the condition it should be in. Our thought life affects our heart. If you were to die today, would people say you had a good heart? Think about the condition of your heart today.

☐ Pray   ☐ Read   Currently working on _____

Evening Reflection

Day 3

"not by works of righteousness which we have done, but according to His mercy He saved us, through the washing of regeneration and renewing of the Holy Spirit,"

Titus 3:5

We are saved by the mercy of God and not our works. There is nothing we can do to be saved other than to ask for Christ to forgive us and be our Savior. Today, live a life that is pleasing to Christ because you want to, not because you think you have to.

☐ Pray   ☐ Read   Currently working on _____

Evening Reflection

Day 4

"but made Himself of no reputation,
taking the form of a bondservant, and coming
in the likeness of men."

Philippians 2:7

How many Kings throughout history have given up their
riches in order to serve others? How many of us would be
willing to give up our reputation in order to be a servant?
Rather than trying to build your reputation or do things that
would look good on a resumé, serve others today.

☐ Pray   ☐ Read   Currently working on _____

Evening Reflection

Day 5

"He who walks with wise men will be wise,
But the companion of fools will be destroyed."

Proverbs 13:20

Do you consider your friends to be wise? Do you act foolishly
while together? Take time today to determine if your friends
act with wisdom or foolishness.

☐ Pray   ☐ Read   Currently working on _____

Evening Reflection

Day 6

"And if it seems evil to you to serve the LORD,
choose for yourselves this day whom you will serve,
whether the gods which your fathers served that were on
the other side of the River, or the gods of the Amorites,
in whose land you dwell. But as for me and my house,
we will serve the LORD."

Joshua 24:15

Choosing who we will serve is a daily occurrence. I guess it is actually a choice-by-choice event. We can start out making choices to serve God, but there's a good chance at some point during the day we are going to choose something that serves ourselves or other gods. Throughout today, think about if the choices you make are serving God.

☐ Pray   ☐ Read   Currently working on _____

Evening Reflection

Day 7

"A quick-tempered man acts foolishly,
And a man of wicked intentions is hated."

Proverbs 14:17

According to this verse, I have spent part of my life foolishly. Today a quick-tempered man would be described as someone with a short fuse. Does this describe you? If so, pray that the Lord will help you be aware of your temper today.

☐ Pray   ☐ Read   Currently working on _____

Evening Reflection

Day 8

"For all the law is fulfilled in one word, even in this:
'You shall love your neighbor as yourself.'"

Galatians 5:14

What would this world be like if we all simply obeyed this one commandment. Our world changes one person at a time. Are you willing to start living out this commandment today?

☐ Pray   ☐ Read   Currently working on _____

Evening Reflection

23

Day 9

"The heart of the righteous studies how to answer,
But the mouth of the wicked pours forth evil."

Proverbs 15:28

How much time do you spend studying your Bible? Not reading it to say you read it, but studying it with a desire to learn? The answers to all of life's questions are in the Bible. It is up to us to search for them. Spend time studying God's letter to you today.

☐ Pray   ☐ Read   Currently working on _____

Evening Reflection

Day 10

"If then you were raised with Christ, seek those things
which are above, where Christ is, sitting at the right hand
of God. Set your mind on things above,
not on things on the earth."

Colossians 3:1-2

Far too often our mind is set on things of this earth. We are
more concerned about riches and fame than we are service
and humility. Evaluate where your mind is set today.

☐ Pray   ☐ Read   Currently working on _____

Evening Reflection

Day 11

"Whoever has no rule over his own spirit Is like a city
broken down, without walls."

Proverbs 25:28

How much control do you have of yourself? How about when
someone cuts you off on the road? What about when you get
to the front of the store to check out and see only two lines
are open? What about when someone bumps into you in the
hallway at school? We should not allow any of these things to
upset us, but we often do. When you start to get angry today,
ask yourself if it is worth it.

☐ Pray   ☐ Read   Currently working on ＿＿＿＿＿＿＿＿＿

Evening Reflection

Day 12

"After these things He went out and saw a tax collector named Levi, sitting at the tax office. And He said to him, 'Follow Me.' So he left all, rose up, and followed Him."

Luke 5:27-28

If Jesus Himself were to walk by you today and say, "Follow Me," would you do it? If you have a relationship with Christ, you are expected to follow Him on a daily basis. Are there things in your life that hinder you from following Christ? Would you be willing to take a pay cut and lose some luxuries in order to follow your Savior? Would you consider moving away from all you know? Evaluate today if there is anything in your life more important to you than following Christ.

☐ Pray　☐ Read　Currently working on _____

Evening Reflection

Day 13

"To do evil is like sport to a fool. But a man of
understanding has wisdom."

Proverbs 10:23

Have you ever done something you knew was wrong just to
see if you could get away with it? There is an addicting thrill
to not getting caught--that is until we start to care about God
seeing everything. Today, do what is pleasing to God rather
than trying not to get caught by man.

☐ Pray ☐ Read Currently working on _____

Evening Reflection

Day 14

"And when he had sent the multitudes away, He went up on the mountain by Himself to pray. Now when evening came, He was alone there."

Matthew 14:23

Jesus Himself sought a place where He could be alone to pray. If the Savior of the world found a place to pray alone, don't you think we should also? Do you have a place you can go to get away and pray? If not, what about the garage, sitting outside, in the shower, or alone in a room. Spend time alone in prayer today and every day.

☐ Pray ☐ Read Currently working on _____

Evening Reflection

Day 15

Toby Mac's song "City on Our Knees" talks about letting
God work in your life starting right now.

Go to www.StumblingServant.com and click on the Morning
Thoughts Song Challenges link, then Day 15. There you will
find a link to the lyrics of this song and another link to listen
to it. Read the lyrics to this song for yourself and determine if
you are willing to accept the challenge they present today.

☐ Pray　　☐ Read　　Currently working on _____

Evening Reflection

Day 16

"Know that the LORD, He is God; It is He who has made us, and not we ourselves; We are His people and the sheep of His pasture."

Psalm 100:3

Sometimes we get the idea that we are self-made or that we pulled ourselves up by our boot straps, but that is not true. The Lord created us, and He has given us everything we have. Give thanks to the Lord today for who He is and for what you have.

☐ Pray ☐ Read Currently working on _____

Evening Reflection

Day 17

"Out of the same mouth proceed blessing and cursing. My brethren, these things ought not to be so."

James 3:10

We use the same mouth that sings and prays to God to talk bad about people and curse without even thinking twice. Why is that so? Everything that comes out of our mouth should honor God. None of us are perfect and we all say things we shouldn't, but we should strive to honor God with everything we say. Start focusing on honoring God with the things that you say today.

☐ Pray   ☐ Read   Currently working on _____

Evening Reflection

Day 18

"Let this mind be in you which was also in Christ Jesus,"

Philippians 2:5

Our first question should be, "What mind was in Christ?"

That question is answered in Philippians 2:2-4. It says "fulfill my joy by being like-minded, having the same love, being of one accord, of one mind. Let nothing be done through selfish ambition or conceit, but in lowliness of mind let each esteem others better than himself. Let each of you look out not only for his own interests, but also for the interests of others."

Is this your mindset, or are you all about living the "American Dream," looking out for number 1, and getting what you believe you've earned? We would be in bad shape if Jesus didn't put others before Himself. Start to develop the mind of Christ today.

☐ Pray   ☐ Read   Currently working on ＿＿＿＿＿＿＿＿

Evening Reflection

Day 19

"For God has not given us a spirit of fear, but of power and of love and of a sound mind."

II Timothy 1:7

Fear is not from the Lord. He does not intend for us to live in fear. Is there something you have been living in fear of? Refuse to let fear control your life today.

☐ Pray   ☐ Read   Currently working on _____

Evening Reflection

Day 20

"You believe that there is one God. You do well. Even the demons believe—and tremble! But do you want to know, O foolish man, that faith without works is dead?"

James 2:19-20

Most people say they believe in God. Back when I was growing up, AOL was the social media giant. Everyone had instant messenger. On the majority of people's AOL profiles was the statement that they "love God." It's the same thing now with Facebook and all the other social networks. It's time we get real and understand if we "love God", then our actions will show it. If a person "loves God," then their FB or Twitter posts should reflect it. If a person "loves God," then how they treat their co-workers, parents, children, teammates, classmates, teachers, friends, and strangers will show it. If you say you "love God," I challenge you to show it. If you do, then people will ask you why you are doing what you are doing and you will have a chance to share the love of Christ with them. Start today by letting your actions show you love God rather than saying it.

☐ Pray ☐ Read Currently working on _____

Evening Reflection

Day 21

"A wise man will hear and increase learning, And a man of understanding will attain wise counsel,"

Proverbs 1:5

How willing are you to learn from other people? Do you have people in your life you consider wise whom you can seek advice from? Today, be willing to listen to other people's input.

☐ Pray   ☐ Read   Currently working on _____

Evening Reflection

Day 22

saying, "Father, if it is Your will, take this cup away from Me; nevertheless not My will, but Yours, be done."

Luke 22:42

To me, this is the ultimate display of trust. Do you think Jesus was happy, joyful, or excited about going to the cross? Of course He wasn't! It says in Luke 22 that He was in agony. Jesus was not in any way looking forward to going to the cross, but he trusted God enough in order to endure all of it. Determine today if you trust God enough to do things His way instead of your way.

☐ Pray   ☐ Read   Currently working on _____

Evening Reflection

Day 23

"Oh God, You know my foolishness;
And my sins are not hidden from You."

Psalm 69:5

God sees everything we do. No one else in the world may know, but God is aware and capable of exposing everything to other people. I've heard it said that if we lived like everything we did would make the front page of the next day's newspaper, we would all live better. What makes tomorrow's headline is up to what you do today. Today, think about the things you are involved in and determine if you would regret anything if it ended up tomorrows headline.

☐ Pray   ☐ Read   Currently working on _____

Evening Reflection

Day 24

"A violent man entices his neighbor,
And leads him in a way that is not good."

Proverbs 16:29

What way are you leading those around you? There are only two ways we can lead others: towards Christ, or away from Him. Make sure all of your actions lead others toward Christ today.

☐ Pray   ☐ Read   Currently working on _____

Evening Reflection

Day 25

"For there is not a just man on earth who does good and
does not sin."

Ecclesiastes 7:20

Think of the best person that you know--the person that you
think never does anything wrong. This verse tells us that we
all sin. Each and every one of us has areas of weakness. Do
you know what your weaknesses are? Today, identify those
areas and ask God to show you the changes you need to
make.

☐ Pray ☐ Read Currently working on _____

Evening Reflection

Day 26

"He who keeps the commandment keeps his soul, But he who is careless of his ways will die."

Proverbs 19:16

How careless are you? Do you have vices in your life that don't seem to be a big deal? Are the things that you do that are not pleasing to God an afterthought in your mind? Today, bury your vices before they bury you relationally, physically, or eternally.

☐ Pray ☐ Read Currently working on _____

Evening Reflection

Day 27

"Do not love sleep, lest you come to poverty; Open your eyes, and you will be satisfied with bread."

Proverbs 20:13

Time is one thing that we can never get back. If we sleep more than we need, we are not being a wise steward of the time God has given us. A person who loves to sleep probably does not love to do much else. Don't sleep today away.

☐ Pray   ☐ Read   Currently working on _____

Evening Reflection

Day 28

Monthly Prayer

Sirens mean that something has gone wrong. Responders could be headed to a car wreck, robbery, fire, domestic violence, murder, bomb threat, or any number of things. Those sirens are for a specific person or persons. It is a very critical time for all involved. Have you ever thought about all who could potentially be involved with the sirens you hear? Some of those include the person/persons involved in the situation, their family and friends, police, firefighters, medics, nurses, surgeons, lawyers, jurors, judges, and prison workers. I would say that the majority of the time we hear sirens before the family and friends of those involved find out something has happened. There are numerous people that we can pray for when we hear sirens. There are also numerous things we can pray for such as safety, comfort, peace, and strength for all those involved. Most importantly we can pray that if anyone involved does not have a relationship with the Lord, that the event would lead them to one and that the Lord would bring good out of the situation. From here on out, be in prayer when you hear sirens.

☐ Pray   ☐ Read   Currently working on _____

Evening Reflection

43

Day 29

"Give unto the Lord the glory due to His name;
Worship the Lord in the beauty of holiness."

Psalm 29:2

In order to give glory to God, we must first realize all that we are and all that we have comes from Him. If we are not thankful for all He has done for us, we will not give Him the glory He deserves. A person who gives God glory in private finds it easier to give God glory in public. Make it a point to give God glory today privately and publicly.

☐ Pray   ☐ Read   Currently working on _____

Evening Reflection

Day 30

Remedy Drive's song "All Along" talks about realizing that Christ is what we have been searching for. We try to fill our lives with all types of stuff, but He is what we need.

Go to www.StumblingServant.com and click on the Morning Thoughts Song Challenges link, then Day 30. There you will find a link to the lyrics of this song and another link so you can listen to it. After you read the lyrics or listen to the song, determine if you are living for the wrong things.

☐ Pray ☐ Read Currently working on _____

Evening Reflection

Day 31

"It is not good to eat much honey; So to seek one's own glory is not glory."

Proverbs 25:27

If you are living a life seeking your own glory, then you aren't living a life that is seeking glory for God. Evaluate whose glory you are seeking today.

☐ Pray ☐ Read Currently working on _____

Evening Reflection

Day 32

"Therefore we also, since we are surrounded by so great a cloud of witnesses, let us lay aside every weight, and the sin which so easily ensnares us, and let us run with endurance the race that is set before us,"

Hebrews 12:1

People are watching you. If others know that you are a Christian, then they are really watching you. What are they seeing? Do you know what weights and sins easily ensnare you? Are you striving with endurance to become the person Christ has called you to be? Make today your first step on that journey, if you are not already on it.

☐ Pray   ☐ Read   Currently working on _____

Evening Reflection

Day 33

"But we are all like an unclean thing, And all our righteousnesses are like filthy rags; We all fade as a leaf, And our iniquities, like the wind, Have taken us away."

Isaiah 64:6

This verse says "we all" twice. How we view ourselves compared to other people is very important. Do you let the things you have accomplished or the way you live your life lead you to believe you are better than others? No matter how little we sin, we are all sinners. Don't allow yourself to look down on anyone else today.

☐ Pray   ☐ Read   Currently working on _____

Evening Reflection

Day 34

"Then Samuel said to the people, 'Do not fear. You have done all this wickedness; yet do not turn aside from following the LORD, but serve the LORD with all your heart.'"

1 Samuel 12:20

The people of Israel realized that asking for a King was not the best thing to do. Samuel responded by asking them to follow the Lord and to serve Him with all their heart. Have there been times in your life when you realized you may not have made the best decision? I know I have made some pretty bad decisions. When we do make poor choices, it is important not to give up. Today, keep your eyes on Christ, serve Him, and push through whatever obstacles may be in your way.

☐ Pray ☐ Read Currently working on _____

Evening Reflection

Day 35

"There is one who speaks like the piercings of a sword, But the tongue of the wise promotes health."

Proverbs 12:18

This seems to go against the old "sticks and stones" saying. Are you a person who wounds the people you talk to, or are you a person whose words build people up? We often unknowingly hurt people by the things we say, but sometimes we say hurtful things and don't care. Today at school, work, in the store, or wherever you go, do not allow yourself to speak words that harm.

☐ Pray   ☐ Read   Currently working on _____

Evening Reflection

Day 36

"But now indeed there are many members,
yet one body. And the eye cannot say to the hand,
'I have no need of you'; nor again the head to the feet,
'I have no need of you.'"

1 Corinthians 12:20-21

What would happen if the professional sports owner told the cleaning crew they were no longer needed? Piles of trash would start to pile up, the bathrooms would be dirty, and soon fans would no longer want to attend games. People want to feel appreciated. No one wants to go to work, school, or practice and never hear someone say, "Good job." As members of the body of Christ we should always go out of our way to make sure those around us feel appreciated. Not just fellow Christians but everyone around us. Today, let those around you know that you truly appreciate them.

☐ Pray   ☐ Read   Currently working on _____

Evening Reflection

Day 37

"The righteous should choose his friends carefully, For the way of the wicked leads them astray."

Proverbs 12:26

This verse applies to all age groups, but I think it is very important to youth and young adults. If we are trying to live like Christ, then the friends we are closest to should be doing the same. This doesn't mean we are to only be friendly to people trying to become more like Christ. It means the people we hang out with in our spare time should be bringing you closer to Christ and not further away from Him. Today, evaluate the friends you spend the most time with and determine if you bring each other closer to Christ.

Through my teenage years I practically grew up at church camp with my friends at Camp Ta-Ku-La. If you are looking for a place to hold an event in East Texas check out their website and see if they can accommodate your needs. www.CampTaKuLa.com

☐ Pray   ☐ Read   Currently working on _____

Evening Reflection

Day 38

"Finally, my brethren, be strong in the Lord and in the power of His might. Put on the whole armor of God, that you may be able to stand against the wiles of the devil. For we do not wrestle against flesh and blood, but against principalities, against powers, against the rulers of the darkness of this age, against spiritual hosts of wickedness in the heavenly places. Therefore take up the whole armor of God, that you may be able to withstand in the evil day, and having done all, to stand. Stand therefore, having girded your waist with truth, having put on the breastplate of righteousness,"

Ephesians 6:10-13,14

This is the first of a few days that cover the armor of God. There is a spiritual war going on. If we go into battle unprepared, how can we expect to survive the daily battles? We are told how to protect ourselves against the evil of this world. Today's focus is on truth and righteousness. Be honest and do the right thing today. Normally we lie when we have messed up or when we want to try to impress others. If you mess up, own up to it. If you want to try to impress others, just remember they won't be impressed when they find out you lie about things. If you are faced with an opportunity to cheat, steal, gossip, lust, or do anything else that isn't right, don't do it. Tell the truth and do the right thing today.

☐ Pray   ☐ Read   Currently working on _____

Evening Reflection

Day 39

"If the world hates you, you know that it hated
Me before it hated you."

John 15:18

Jesus was not a popular person with everyone. He was very
polarizing. Some people loved Him, but others hated Him.
If you live for Jesus, there will be some that hate you. Pray
for them and be kind to them. If you experience hate today,
respond with the love of Christ.

☐ Pray   ☐ Read   Currently working on _____

Evening Reflection

Day 40

"Examine me, O LORD, and prove me;
Try my mind and my heart."

Psalm 26:2

If your mind and heart were to go on trial today, what would
the verdict be? Would you be guilty of living for Christ or
acquitted? Pray today, and every day, that the Lord would
examine you and convict you about aspects of your life you
need to change.

☐ Pray   ☐ Read   Currently working on _____

Evening Reflection

Day 41

"Better a poor and wise youth Than an old and foolish king who will be admonished no more."

Ecclesiastes 4:13

"Wise youth." I hope this verse encourages any youth or young adults. You may not be popular, you may not be rich, you may not be the most athletic, but you can be wise. I hope this verse reminds the rest of us that youth are of value and that we are never too old to be corrected. Be wise today.

☐ Pray   ☐ Read   Currently working on _____

Evening Reflection

Day 42

"The way of a fool is right in his own eyes,
But he who heeds counsel is wise."

Proverbs 12:15

There is a difference in seeking counsel and heeding counsel. Have you ever sought advice from someone, but then did not like what they had to say? You can seek counsel without heeding it. Sometimes we have good intentions but allow ourselves to get to the point where we won't listen to anything anyone around us has to say. Be sure you are not in that place today.

☐ Pray   ☐ Read   Currently working on _____

Evening Reflection

Day 43

"A good name is to be chosen rather than great riches,
Loving favor rather than silver and gold."

Proverbs 22:1

Do you know anyone who would sacrifice their good name in order to get rich? The news is full of people selling themselves out while chasing money. If we aren't careful, we can do this without even realizing it. Have you ever made a scene over being charged too much at the store? Have you ever called to complain about a bill and been disrespectful? No matter how much money is at stake, we need to act in a way that reflects well on our name. The actions you take today will reflect on your name and your testimony. Make sure they reflect positively.

☐ Pray   ☐ Read   Currently working on _____

Evening Reflection

Day 44

"For there is no partiality with God."

Romans 2:11

God does not show partiality to any person. This means no person has an advantage over another. Did God give the people we consider to be spiritual giants more than He gave us? No. God does not care who does His work. He equips those that are willing to do it. Be willing to do God's work today, and take a step toward becoming a spiritual giant.

☐ Pray   ☐ Read   Currently working on _____

Evening Reflection

Day 45

John Newton's song "Amazing Grace" is known by many people. The Grace of God truly is amazing.

Go to www.StumblingServant.com and click on the Morning Thoughts Song Challenges link, then Day 45. There you will find a link to the lyrics of "Amazing Grace." After you read the lyrics, determine if you have been living as if you have been found and received your sight.

☐ Pray   ☐ Read   Currently working on _____

Evening Reflection

Day 46

"Indeed we count them blessed who endure.
You have heard of the perseverance of Job and seen
the end intended by the Lord—that the Lord is very
compassionate and merciful."

James 5:11

No matter how bad we have it, it's hard to imagine any of us experiencing more pain than Job. If you are going through tough times, remember that the Lord is compassionate and merciful. Look to Him, stay faithful, and endure. If you aren't going through tough times, be thankful and try to help someone who is. No matter where you are today, press on.

☐ Pray   ☐ Read   Currently working on _____

Evening Reflection

Day 47

"For what I am doing, I do not understand. For what I will to do, that I do not practice; but what I hate, that I do."

Romans 7:15

In other words, I always find myself not doing the things I want to do and doing the things I don't want to do. Sound familiar? I know it does to me. We all have things that we struggle with, but we overcome them in different ways. The one constant is that we all must admit that we cannot overcome it on our own. We must rely on God's strength. Whatever it is that you do that you don't want to, or don't do that you want to do, give it to God today and allow Him to show His strength though your weakness.

☐ Pray   ☐ Read   Currently working on _____

Evening Reflection

Day 48

"Therefore, to him who knows to do good and
does not do it, to him it is sin."

James 4:17

Too often we focus on not doing the things we shouldn't do.
We seem to understand that doing the things we shouldn't
do is sin, but we have a hard time understanding that not
doing what we should do is sin as well. We know we shouldn't
talk about others, but we don't talk about His love with other
people. We know we shouldn't steal, but we don't give to
others. We know we shouldn't put other things before God,
but we don't spend time with Him. Do what you know you
should do today.

☐ Pray   ☐ Read   Currently working on _____

Evening Reflection

Day 49

This is the day the LORD has made;
We will rejoice and be glad in it."

Psalm 118:24

No matter what happened yesterday, or what will happen later on today, claim this verse. Be joyful today that the Lord has blessed you with another day.

☐ Pray   ☐ Read   Currently working on _____

Evening Reflection

_____

_____

_____

_____

_____

_____

_____

_____

65

Day 50

"My voice You shall hear in the morning, O LORD; in the morning will I direct it to you, and I will look up."

Psalm 5:3

Do you start your days off with prayer? Do you thank God for another day? Do you ask the Lord to help you do the things you should do and not the things you shouldn't do? Do you ask Him to help you hold yourself to His standards and not the world's? Do you tell Him you want to live for Him and not for yourself? Do you ask Him to help you show other people His love? Start today off with prayer.

☐ Pray   ☐ Read   Currently working on _____

Evening Reflection

Day 51

"You shall love the LORD your God with all your heart, with all your soul, and with all your strength."

Deuteronomy 6:5

Everything about us is an offering to God. Today, strive to be a pleasing offering to Him in all you do.

☐ Pray   ☐ Read   Currently working on _____

Evening Reflection

Day 52

"He who answers a matter before he hears it,
It is folly and shame to him."

Proverbs 18:13

How often do we chime in with our two cents before we even know the whole story? It is easy to hear one thing and jump to a conclusion, but, as many of us know, doing so can bring shame. Before you offer your opinion on something today, make sure you have all the facts.

☐ Pray   ☐ Read   Currently working on _____

Evening Reflection

Day 53

"He who is slow to wrath has great understanding,
But he who is impulsive exalts folly."

Proverbs 14:29

Are you quick to turn your wrath loose on others?
Do you act before you know the facts of a situation? If you
do, odds are you have made a fool of yourself once or twice.
Seek to understand situations today instead of reacting with
impulse.

☐ Pray   ☐ Read   Currently working on _____

Evening Reflection

Day 54

"The refining pot is for silver and the furnace for gold,
But the LORD tests the hearts."

Proverbs 17:3

In order for silver and gold to be purified, they must be melted. This requires extremely high temperatures. After melted, they can be poured into molds to make the finished products we see. In order for us to become more like Christ, we must be melted down and poured into His mold. This process is much easier when we are willing participants. Ask God to work on your heart today.

☐ Pray   ☐ Read   Currently working on _____

Evening Reflection

Day 55

"What is desired in a man is kindness,
And a poor man is better than a liar."

Proverbs 19:22

Most of us find it pretty easy to be kind to our friends, but what about our parents, siblings, spouses, children, co-workers, and strangers? We often find ourselves being disrespectful to the people closest to us who are more than friends. We pass it off as the norm, but should it be? Today, treat everyone around you like you do your best friends.

☐ Pray   ☐ Read   Currently working on _____

Evening Reflection

Day 56

When you are driving, how often do you pass people who are walking, running, or riding a bike? I would guess we don't even notice them most of the time. Our main concern when we do see them is probably that they don't drift out into the road in front of us. From now on, when you see someone walking, running, or riding a bike, pray for them. Pray that they make it to wherever it is that they are going safely. Pray that other drivers who pass them will see them.

☐ Pray   ☐ Read   Currently working on _____

Evening Reflection

Day 57

"Lying lips are an abomination to the LORD,
But those who deal truthfully are His delight."

Proverbs 12:22

Today, we are all faced with the choice to be an abomination to the Lord or to be His delight. Choose truth over lies today.

□ Pray   □ Read   Currently working on _____

Evening Reflection

Day 58

"Therefore be merciful, just as your Father is merciful."

Luke 6:36

Merciful is a word we don't hear very often in our everyday language. Just to clarify, it is not the same thing as grace. Grace is getting something good we don't deserve, and mercy is not getting something bad we do deserve. God shows us grace by allowing us to go to Heaven if we accept Christ as our Savior; whereas, He also shows us mercy by not sending us all to Hell, even though we are sinners and deserve it. Today, think about how merciful you are as a person. Can you remember the last time you showed someone mercy?

☐ Pray   ☐ Read   Currently working on _____

Evening Reflection

Day 59

"When I consider Your heavens, the work of Your fingers, the moon and the stars, which You have ordained. What is man that you are mindful of him, And the son of man that You visit him?"

Psalm 8:3-4

We admire the stars, moon, mountains, sunsets, and other natural wonders God has created, but He is more concerned with us. We would rather travel and see what we believe to be God's most beautiful creations than invest in what God sees as His most beautiful creations. His masterpieces live in your house, live next door to you, go to your school, work with you, are in jails, and are in hospitals. Choose to see those around you today as masterpieces of God.

☐ Pray   ☐ Read   Currently working on _____

Evening Reflection

Day 60

Third Day's song "God of Wonders" talks about how the universe itself is a reflection of God's majesty.

Go to www.StumblingServant.com and click on the Morning Thoughts Song Challenges link, then Day 60. There you will find links to read the lyrics to this song and to listen to it. There is also a video of Third Day performing this song posted to the page. After you read the lyrics or watch the performance, take time to find some pictures of our galaxy and universe. Today, remember that the Creator of the pictures you see created you also. Next time you are able, look at the stars and be in awe of their Creator.

☐ Pray   ☐ Read   Currently working on _____

Evening Reflection

Day 61

"My brethren, do not hold the faith of our Lord Jesus
Christ, the Lord of glory, with partiality."

James 2:1

Are you partial with whom you show the love of Christ?
It is much easier to help out those we know compared to
strangers, but God did not call us to show His love only to the
people we know. We are to reach out to the poor, the proud,
the sick, the strong, the weak, the wealthy, the rejected, the
respected, and all that fall in between. I don't deserve the
love of Christ any more than the worst criminal one could
imagine, and neither do you. Don't be partial as to who you
share the love of Christ with today.

☐ Pray   ☐ Read   Currently working on _____

Evening Reflection

Day 62

"And whatever you do, do it heartily,
as to the Lord and not to men,"

Colossians 3:23

What are your plans for today? Maybe you have to do
something you aren't looking forward to doing. Maybe
you're just doing the same old thing. Whatever it is, find joy
in knowing that the Lord is watching and wants you to do
it the best you can. Today, put forth your best effort, even if
you don't want to.

☐ Pray   ☐ Read   Currently working on _____

Evening Reflection

Day 63

"Your word I have hidden in my heart,
That I might not sin against You."

Psalm 119:11

Is this true for you? I know I fall very short in this area of my faith. Do you have more scripture memorized or song lyrics? What about movie lines, formulas, phone numbers, credit card numbers, or driving directions? What is something you struggle with? Find a verse today that can help you in that area and memorize it by the end of the week.

☐ Pray   ☐ Read   Currently working on _____

Evening Reflection

Day 64

"Do you see a man wise in his own eyes?
There is more hope for a fool than for him."

Proverbs 26:12

Do you think you have "arrived?" If so, this verse is talking about you. No matter how much God allows us to accomplish, we have to realize it is only through Him we are able to do anything. Even with God's help, we still have flaws. Today, don't act like you know it all because none of us do.

☐ Pray   ☐ Read   Currently working on _____

Evening Reflection

Day 65

"Brethren, I do not count myself to have apprehended; but one thing I do, forgetting those things which are behind and reaching forward to those things which are ahead,"

Philippians 3:13

When we hold on to what we have done in the past, whether good or bad, we can not put our all into the present. Today is a new day regardless of if you won the Super Bowl yesterday or failed a science exam. No matter what you did yesterday, last week, last month, or last year, forget about it and focus on doing what you need to today to get where you want to be tomorrow.

☐ Pray   ☐ Read   Currently working on _____

Evening Reflection

Day 66

"So the LORD said to Joshua: Get up!
Why do you lie thus on your face?"

Joshua 7:10

This verse is one of the reasons I am glad my parents gave me the name Joshua. Feel free to insert your name and recall it in times of discouragement. No matter what you are going through, the Lord did not call us to be defeated. Through Him we are victorious. Pick yourself up off of the floor today and live by faith.

☐ Pray   ☐ Read   Currently working on _____

Evening Reflection

Day 67

"Do not be afraid of sudden terror, Nor of trouble from the wicked when it comes; For the LORD will be your confidence, And will keep your foot from being caught."

Proverbs 3:25-26

Fear can result from something unexpected taking place. Terrorists and thieves don't announce their plans to their victims. If they did, they would lose the element of surprise. The good news is the Lord is not surprised by anything. He knows the choices people will make before they make them. Be confident in the Lord today if faced with the opportunity to be afraid.

☐ Pray   ☐ Read   Currently working on _____

Evening Reflection

Day 68

"Trust in the LORD with all your heart, And lean not on your own understanding; In all your ways acknowledge Him, And He shall direct your paths."

Proverbs 3:5-6

Have you ever been in a situation where you just didn't understand what was going on? Rest assured that you are not alone. It is not our responsibility to understand everything that happens in our lives. It is our responsibility to trust in the Lord 100% and to live for Him in everything we do. If we do that, then He will guide us. Today, determine how much your life reflects that you trust the Lord.

☐ Pray   ☐ Read   Currently working on _____

Evening Reflection

Day 69

"The tongue of the righteous is choice silver;
The heart of the wicked is worth little."

Proverbs 10:20

A righteous tongue is worth more than a wicked heart.
Is your tongue closer to being silver than your heart is to
being worth little? Today, strive to speak with a tongue that
is pleasing to the Lord.

☐ Pray   ☐ Read   Currently working on _____

Evening Reflection

Day 70

"A satisfied soul loathes the honeycomb, But to a hungry soul every bitter thing is sweet."

Proverbs 27:7

Are you satisfied or hungry? Are you the one to complain when the lunch lady gives you one big slice of pizza and a small one instead of two big slices? Do you walk to a pantry full of food and complain that there is nothing to eat? Are you only willing to help out if you are in the spotlight? Do you provide places you will be speaking/singing with a food and beverage list? Don't live your life as a picky person. Today, appreciate the things that come your way as you would if you were starving.

☐ Pray   ☐ Read   Currently working on _____

Evening Reflection

Day 71

"Deliver those who are drawn toward death, And hold
back those stumbling to the slaughter."

Proverbs 24:11

Do you have friends who are taking risks they don't need
to be taking? Maybe they are using drugs, thinking about
cheating on their spouse, or involved in crimes. Have you
taken time to talk with them about the things they are doing?
Not talk *to* them, but talk *with* them. God does not want us
to condemn other people, but we do need to talk with them
out of love if we know something they are involved in is
dangerous. If you know someone who is stumbling toward
death, reach out to them in love today.

☐ Pray ☐ Read Currently working on _____

Evening Reflection

Day 72

"Therefore love the stranger, for you were strangers in
the land of Egypt."

Deuteronomy 10:19

Be kind to someone that you do not know today. Look for
someone that needs encouragement.

☐ Pray   ☐ Read   Currently working on _____

Evening Reflection

Day 73

"'But why do you call Me 'Lord, Lord,'
and not do the things which I say?'"

Luke 6:46

If we call ourselves Christians but do not do the things Christ
commands us to do, then why do we consider ourselves
Christians? Live a life obedient to Christ today.

☐ Pray   ☐ Read   Currently working on _____

Evening Reflection

Day 74

"The foolishness of a man twists his way,
And his heart frets against the Lord."

Proverbs 19:3

Have you allowed your ways to be twisted? It is easy to compare yourself to others and say, "I'm not doing this or doing that," but any wrongdoing is displeasing to our Lord. Today, examine your life to see if you have allowed yourself to do things you used to not do.

☐ Pray   ☐ Read   Currently working on _____

Evening Reflection

Day 75

Casting Crowns' song "Slow Fade" is a great description of how we often end up getting ourselves into trouble because we gave in to the little things.

Go to www.StumblingServant.com and click on the Morning Thoughts Song Challenges link, then Day 75. There you will find links to read the lyrics to this song, listen to the song, and watch the music video for the song. Reflect on your life and determine if you are in the midst of a slow fade today.

☐ Pray ☐ Read Currently working on _____

Evening Reflection

Day 76

"No one can serve two masters; for either he will hate the one and love the other, or else he will be loyal to the one and despise the other. You cannot serve God and mammon."

Matthew 6:24

Mammon means material wealth or material possessions. Have you been serving God or things of this world? What have you done to serve God lately? Today, determine who you are serving.

☐ Pray ☐ Read Currently working on _____

Evening Reflection

Day 77

"A wise son heeds his father's instruction,
But a scoffer does not listen to rebuke."

Proverbs 13:1

Do you listen to instruction? Do you listen when someone corrects you? Today, be willing to accept both instruction and correction.

☐ Pray   ☐ Read   Currently working on _____

Evening Reflection

Day 78

"For no other foundation can anyone lay than that which is laid, which is Jesus Christ."

1 Corinthians 3:11

What is the foundation of your life? When it comes down to it, what is the most important thing to you? What do you wake up in the morning for? What is your drive and motivation? Is it to become a millionaire? What if you lose all your money? Is it to marry the most attractive spouse? What if your spouse dies? Is it to have great children? What if your children end up in jail? Is it to become a CEO? What if the company folds? If any of these things are your foundation, then one way or another your foundation is going to crack. Jesus Christ is the only thing in this world that will not change. If He is your foundation, then you will be able to withstand the trials listed above along with any others a person could endure. Evaluate the condition of your foundation today.

☐ Pray   ☐ Read   Currently working on _____

Evening Reflection

Day 79

"I can do all things through Christ who strengthens me."

Philippians 4:13

Does Christ strengthen you? Do you allow Him to strengthen you? When do you allow Him to strengthen you? Sunday mornings? Sunday nights? What about Wednesday nights? If these are the only times Christ strengthens us, then we are probably pretty spiritually weak. In order to be strengthened by Christ, we must seek after Him. We must spend time in prayer and reading His Word. Claiming this verse during difficult times will do no good if we do not allow Him to strengthen us daily. Allow Christ to strengthen you today by spending time with him.

☐ Pray   ☐ Read   Currently working on _____

Evening Reflection

Day 80

"For I am not ashamed of the gospel of Christ, for it is the power of God to salvation for everyone who believes, for the Jew first and also for the Greek"

Romans 1:16

Have you ever been ashamed of something? Most of us are ashamed of certain things we have done in our lives, but what about being ashamed of something you shouldn't be ashamed of. I know I haven't always been the boldest for Christ. How can we be ashamed of something that can provide salvation to all those we come into contact with? It is our duty to live a shameless life for Christ. Live for Christ today, and don't be ashamed of doing it.

☐ Pray ☐ Read Currently working on _____

Evening Reflection

Day 81

"Do not turn to idols, nor make for yourselves molded gods: I am the Lord your God."

Leviticus 19:4

Do you have any idols in your life? It could be your husband, wife, son, daughter, mom, dad, an athlete, religious leader, boyfriend, girlfriend, actor, actress, model, car, house, boat, computer, or even yourself. Anything we put before Christ is an idol. We must make sure that our relationship with Him is what's most important to us. Keep track of how you spend your time today, and take time tonight to look back and determine if God was the recipient of your worship.

☐ Pray   ☐ Read   Currently working on _____

Evening Reflection

Day 82

"There is one Lawgiver, who is able to save and to destroy. Who are you to judge another?"

James 4:12

When the opportunity to judge someone comes along today, remember that you are not the Lawgiver this verse is referring to.

☐ Pray   ☐ Read   Currently working on _____

Evening Reflection

Day 83

"Let no one say when he is tempted, 'I am tempted by God'; for God cannot be tempted by evil, nor does He Himself tempt anyone. But each one is tempted when he is drawn away by his own desires and enticed."

James 1:13-14

Temptation starts in our mind. When we allow ourselves to think like the world instead of like God, then we are in trouble. Today, when temptation enters your mind, be strong enough to humble yourself and ask Christ for help.

☐ Pray   ☐ Read   Currently working on _____

Evening Reflection

Day 84

Monthly Prayer

When it rains, pray that the Lord would pour out His blessings on the missionaries around the world who have sacrificed their comfort to serve Him in other places. Ask the Lord to give them good heath, to encourage those that may be discouraged, to help them see progress in the people they are working with, to give them fruit for their labor, to meet their needs, and to bless them beyond anything they could ever ask for or imagine.

☐ Pray   ☐ Read   Currently working on _____

Evening Reflection

Day 85

"How much better to get wisdom than gold! And to get understanding is to be chosen rather than silver."

Proverbs 16:16

Where do wisdom and understanding fall on your wish list? Are they ahead of gold and things of this world? Today, determine if the wisdom and understanding of the Lord are more desirable to you than gold and silver.

☐ Pray ☐ Read Currently working on _____

Evening Reflection

Day 86

"A perverse man sows strife, And a whisperer
separates the best of friends."

Proverbs 16:28

We have all whispered things hoping that someone didn't
hear us. It could be because we are going to surprise a
friend with something, but most of the time we aren't saying
anything good. If you feel you need to whisper something to
someone today so the person you are talking about doesn't
hear, just keep it to yourself.

☐ Pray   ☐ Read   Currently working on _____

Evening Reflection

Day 87

"Continue earnestly in prayer, being vigilant in it
with thanksgiving;"

Colossians 4:2

To continue in prayer means you had to already start praying.
How is your prayer life? Do you have a prayer life? Do you
pray multiple times a day, or just when you need something?
When praying, do you take time to thank the Lord for what
He has given you, or do you spend the entire time asking
for things? Spend time in prayer today and don't limit it to
before you eat.

☐ Pray   ☐ Read   Currently working on _____

Evening Reflection

Day 88

"Which of you by worrying can add one cubit
to his stature?"

Matthew 6:27

What do you control other than yourself? Nothing. Who controls everything? God. Today focus on doing your part and leave the rest to Him.

☐ Pray ☐ Read   Currently working on _____

Evening Reflection

Day 89

"I have been crucified with Christ; it is no longer I who live, but Christ lives in me; and the life which I now live in the flesh I live by faith in the Son of God, who loved me and gave Himself for me."

Galatians 2:20

If you have accepted Christ as your Savior, then your life is no longer about you. Giving our life to Christ is not a "Get Out of Hell Free" card. It is a lifelong journey to become more like Him and to lead others to Him. Today, evaluate your willingness to sacrifice the things you want to do for the things He wants you to do.

☐ Pray   ☐ Read   Currently working on _____

Evening Reflection

Day 90

Chris and Conrad's song "Lead Me To The Cross" is a call for Christ to help us live for Him and not for ourselves.

Go to www.StumblingServant.com and click on the Morning Thoughts Song Challenges link, then Day 90. There you will find links to read the lyrics to the song and to listen to it. Acknowledge that you are Christ's today by living out this song.

☐ Pray ☐ Read Currently working on _____

Evening Reflection

Day 91

"Humble yourselves in the sight of the Lord,
and He will lift you up."

James 4:10

Sometimes we seem to have everything going for us, yet we still feel empty. Most of the time it's because we are focused on the wrong things, which means our priorities are out of order. When this happens, we have to humble ourselves before the Lord and make things right. If we do that and keep our priorities straight, then He will lift us up. Humble yourself before the Lord today.

☐ Pray   ☐ Read   Currently working on ＿＿＿＿＿＿

Evening Reflection

Day 92

"Where there is no counsel, the people fall; But in the multitude of counselors there is safety."

Proverbs 11:14

How many people do you have in your life that you can seek advice from? Are they people you would consider to be wise? Will they tell you what you want to hear, or will they be straightforward with you? Do others come to you for counsel? Today, determine if you have quality people in your life you can seek counsel from and if you are preparing yourself to offer wise counsel to others.

☐ Pray   ☐ Read   Currently working on _____

Evening Reflection

Day 93

"And which of you, having a servant plowing or tending sheep, will say to him when he has come in from the field, 'Come at once and sit down to eat'? But will he not rather say to him, 'Prepare something for my supper, and gird yourself and serve me till I have eaten and drunk, and afterward you will eat and drink'? Does he thank that servant because he did the things that were commanded him? I think not. So likewise you, when you have done all those things which you are commanded, say, 'We are unprofitable servants. We have done what was our duty to do.'"

Luke 17:7-10

My dad has had a framed sheet of paper hanging in his house that says "Duty, do" for the last 15-20 years. It's something he came up with himself. I never really put much thought into it until this past year. It's simple, but it says so much. Those of us that are Christians have the duty to do what the Lord has commanded us to do. Today, "Duty, do."

☐ Pray ☐ Read Currently working on _____

Evening Reflection

Day 94

"Cease from anger, and forsake wrath;
Do not fret—it only causes harm."

Psalm 37:8

According to this verse, harm is all that comes from worry. So why is it that we struggle so much with it? Choose to be worry-free today.

☐ Pray   ☐ Read   Currently working on _____

Evening Reflection

110

Day 95

"For you, brethren, have been called to liberty; only do not use liberty as an opportunity for the flesh, but through love serve one another."

Galatians 5:13

The Lord has given us freedom. We have the choice to do what we want to do. This verse is telling us to resist the temptations of the flesh, even though we are free to give in to them. It also tells us to serve each other in love. If we truly love others, then we will want to do things for them. Serve someone in love today.

☐ Pray   ☐ Read   Currently working on _____

Evening Reflection

Day 96

"The highway of the upright is to depart from evil; He who keeps his way preserves his soul."

Proverbs 16:17

"Depart" and "keeps" are key words in this verse. "Depart" tells us that we will face evil, but that it is our job to flee from it. "Keeps" tells us that there will be a chance to give in to the ways of the world. None of us are exempt from temptation. Everyone, from Jesus to you, has been tempted. I would bet the people you view as spiritual giants are the ones that have departed from evil and kept their way more than most. Today, stay away from evil and walk in the way of Christ.

☐ Pray   ☐ Read   Currently working on _____

Evening Reflection

Day 97

"Even a child is known by his deeds, Whether what he does is pure and right."

Proverbs 20:11

We aren't known by our words, but rather by what our actions say. When you see a piece of trash on the ground do you pass it by or bend down and pick it up? Do you hold the door open for the person right behind you or hurry on your way? If we are willing to take time and do the little things, then doing the big things will become second nature. Go the extra mile today to make sure your actions speak well of you.

☐ Pray   ☐ Read   Currently working on _____

Evening Reflection

Day 98

"So husbands ought to love their own wives as their own bodies; he who loves his wife loves himself."

Ephesians 5:28

"Wives, likewise, be submissive to your own husbands, that even if some do not obey the word, they, without a word, may be won by the conduct of their wives,"

1 Peter 3:1

"A wise son makes a glad father, But a foolish son is the grief of his mother."

Proverbs 10:1

Husbands – Do you love your wife as your own body? Think about how important your body is. We often take it for granted until something goes wrong. You never realize how important your big toe or thumb is until you hurt one of them. Those who take care of their body are rewarded by it. Do you take care of your wife? Do you view her as an extension of yourself? Do you realize how important she is to you? Think about all your wife does and take care of her today.

Wives – Does your husband have a relationship with Christ? If not, it is extremely important that they see you live out your faith. Notice the verse says by "conduct" and not by "words." You can not persuade someone into a relationship with Christ. If you do, then odds are it is not a true relationship. Let your actions speak to your husband, and pray that God will work on his heart. Today, serve your husband, not out of weakness, but out of strength knowing that the Lord will use it for good.

Children – Would others say you are wise or foolish? Do your choices make your parents glad or bring them grief? Your actions have a direct impact on your parents. Sometimes we think that the things we do only affect us. We think that people should not think any differently about our parents based on our actions. Neither one of those thoughts are true. Our actions affect all of those around us, and there are a lot of people, even though it is not right, who will look down on our parents for the bad choices we make. Before you do something, ask yourself if it is foolish. Kids who aren't foolish will make their parents glad and won't bring them grief. Be wise today.

☐ Pray   ☐ Read   Currently working on _____

Evening Reflection

Day 99

"He who goes about as a talebearer reveals secrets;
Therefore do not associate with one who
flatters with his lips."

Proverbs 20:19

Are you the type of person who always spews out what you
have heard? If a friend comes to talk to you about something
important to them, can they be confident you wont go tell
other people? If you hear something about someone you
don't care for, do you quickly share it with someone else?
Don't be a talebearer today.

☐ Pray ☐ Read Currently working on _____

Evening Reflection

Day 100

"Riches do not profit in the day of wrath,
But righteousness delivers from death."

Proverbs 11:4

Which is of more value to you, righteousness or riches?
Which one do you invest in more? Which one do you spend
more time working toward? Take time today to evaluate
which of these is more important to you.

☐ Pray   ☐ Read   Currently working on _____

Evening Reflection

Day 101

"For the wages of sin is death, but the gift of God is eternal life in Christ Jesus our Lord."

Romans 6:23

We all deserve death, or eternal separation from God, because we are all sinners. The good news is Jesus offers us the gift of eternal life with Him in Heaven. All we have to do to accept His gift is understand that we are a sinner, believe that Jesus came to die on the cross for our sins and to rise again, and ask Him to forgive us of our sins and become Lord of our life. The choice is ours. Have you accepted His gift? If you haven't, turn to page 11 to learn more about beginning a relationship with Christ.

☐ Pray   ☐ Read   Currently working on _____

Evening Reflection

Day 102

"Let the words of my mouth, and the meditation of my heart, be acceptable in Your sight, O LORD, my strength and my Redeemer."

Psalm 19:14

Often, we claim things that are disproved by our actions. If the Lord is our strength and Redeemer, then we should want our words and thoughts to be acceptable to Him. Use your words and thoughts today to determine if you can truly claim Him as your strength and Redeemer.

☐ Pray   ☐ Read   Currently working on _____

Evening Reflection

Day 103

"A soft answer turns away wrath,
But a harsh word stirs up anger."

Proverbs 15:1

Do your words bring calm in the midst of a storm, or do they create waves? A tense situation can be diffused or escalated. Today, focus on turning away wrath rather than stirring up anger.

☐ Pray   ☐ Read   Currently working on _____

Evening Reflection

Day 104

"The lazy man will not plow because of winter;
He will beg during harvest and have nothing."

Proverbs 20:4

We can always find an excuse not to do something we know
we need to do. It isn't that we always say, "I'm not going to
do it," but we often say, "I'll do it later." Procrastination does
not lead to preparation. No matter how cold this season of
life may be, determine today that you will do what you need
to do to prepare for your future.

☐ Pray   ☐ Read   Currently working on _____

Evening Reflection

Day 105

Matthew West's song "The Motions" sums up how a lot of
us Christians are living these days.

Go to www.StumblingServant.com and click on the Morning
Thoughts Song Challenges link, then Day 105. There you will
find links to read the lyrics, listen to the song, and watch the
music video for the song. After reading the lyrics, listening
to the song, or watching the performance, determine not to
go through the motions today.

☐ Pray   ☐ Read   Currently working on _____

Evening Reflection

Day 106

"Do not rejoice when your enemy falls, And do not let
your heart be glad when he stumbles;"

Proverbs 24:17

Don't be happy when someone who has hurt you goes
through difficult times. Don't get joy out of another student's
failures. Don't get pleasure out of a difficult co-worker going
through hard times. We should hurt for those around us who
are stumbling through difficult times rather than say, "They
got what they deserved." I am guilty of doing this. Today,
work toward having a heart that is sympathetic toward
everyone and not just those you are close to.

☐ Pray   ☐ Read   Currently working on _____

Evening Reflection

123

Day 107

"...Do not sorrow, for the joy of the LORD
is your strength."

Nehemiah 8:10

Is the joy of the Lord your strength? What exactly is the joy of the Lord? I am not a Bible scholar, but to me this verse is saying that instead of worrying about what is going on, we can have joy that God is in control of everything and can draw strength from knowing that. Today, live in the joy of the Lord.

☐ Pray　　☐ Read　　Currently working on _____

Evening Reflection

Day 108

"Listen to this, O Job; Stand still and consider the wondrous works of God."

Job 37:14

Being still is hard for some people to do. I don't necessarily have trouble being physically still all the time, but I have trouble being mentally still. It seems as if my mind is always going, and it is hard to just be still and listen. The pace of life in our world these days is crazy. We all have 24 hours in a day, yet we find it hard to sit still and listen or just look around and admire the things God created. Evaluate how much time you spend being still each day. Make today the first day on a journey of taking time to be still and consider the works of God that surround you.

☐ Pray ☐ Read Currently working on _____

Evening Reflection

Day 109

"just as the Son of Man did not come to be served, but to serve, and to give His life a ransom for many."

Matthew 20:28

What are you doing to serve others? I guess a better question is what are you doing to serve others outside of your church walls? What impact would Christ have made if He only served within the walls of places of worship? Today, look for an area in your community where you can serve.

☐ Pray   ☐ Read   Currently working on _____

Evening Reflection

Day 110

"If then God so clothes the grass, which today is in the field and tomorrow is thrown into the oven, how much more will He clothe you, O you of little faith?"

Luke 12:28

We may not throw grass into ovens these days, but God still provides for us just as He did for the people in Biblical times. Have you ever noticed that even the smallest events have the ability to cause all sorts of worry? They have that ability because we give it to them. It is up to us whether or not we stress over things. Today, make sure you live a life reflective of someone who knows God will provide for them.

☐ Pray   ☐ Read   Currently working on _____

Evening Reflection

Day 111

"Imitate me, just as I also imitate Christ"

1 Corinthians 11:1

Would people be imitating Christ if they imitated you? If people imitated you, would their actions on Sunday be different than Monday –Saturday? Would their speech be pleasing to God? Would the things they talk about be things Christ would talk about? I believe, as many others have said, that we are the only Bible some people will ever read. It is up to you what those around you will read today.

☐ Pray   ☐ Read   Currently working on _____

Evening Reflection

Day 112

Monthly Prayer

How many times do you drive past an American flag each day? If none, then you should think about hanging one at your house. We should see our flag each day to remind us of those who have made sacrifices and who currently are making sacrifices. From now on, when you see an American flag, thank the Lord for all of the men and women who have fought and are fighting to protect our freedom. Ask the Lord to comfort those who are away from their families and to comfort their families as well. Ask the Lord to give strength to those who need it. Ask the Lord to bless those who have served, are serving, and are preparing to serve.

☐ Pray   ☐ Read   Currently working on _____

Evening Reflection

Day 113

"And suddenly, a woman who had a flow of blood for twelve years came from behind and touched the hem of His garment. For she said to herself, 'If only I may touch His garment, I shall be made well.'"

Matthew 9:20-21

Would you have enough faith to reach out and touch the hem of His garment? Would you have enough faith to go to where you knew He was going to be? We are in need of healing in so many areas of our life, yet we refuse to go to the Healer. How often do we truly reach out to God with our problems? No matter what you are going through, no matter how big or how small, no matter how significant or insignificant you may think it is, go to the Healer today and touch His garment.

☐ Pray   ☐ Read   Currently working on _____

Evening Reflection

Day 114

"And in vain they worship Me, Teaching as doctrines the commandments of men."

Mark 7:7

Do you ever question things you are told, or do you usually just take others at their word? We need to research the things we hear. Just as in Bible times, there are people today that preach things as truth that are far from truth. Take time today to determine if you are following others blindly.

☐ Pray   ☐ Read   Currently working on _____

Evening Reflection

Day 115

"Beloved, if God so loved us, we also ought to love one another."

1 John4:11

Who are we not to love each other when God, who is greater than us, loves us? God loves you. Think about that for a minute. Now try to justify not loving another human. Today, become aware of the people you may have a hard time loving and start working on it.

☐ Pray ☐ Read Currently working on _____

Evening Reflection

Day 116

"A scoffer does not love one who corrects him,
Nor will he go to the wise."

Proverbs 15:12

How do you feel about people who justly correct you? Are
you willing to seek the help of others? Today, evaluate how
defensive you are when people that care about you justly
correct you.

☐ Pray   ☐ Read   Currently working on _____

Evening Reflection

Day 117

"For I, the LORD your God, will hold your right hand,
Saying to you, 'Fear not, I will help you.;'"

Isaiah 41:13

Either our God is a liar or He is going to help us. It is up to us to continue to hold His hand in trust or to pull away and try to do things our own way. Cling to His hand and have no fear today.

☐ Pray   ☐ Read   Currently working on ＿＿＿＿＿＿＿

Evening Reflection

Day 118

"And when you pray, you shall not be like the hypocrites. For they love to pray standing in the synagogues and on the corners of the streets, that they may be seen by men. Assuredly, I say to you, they have their reward."

Matthew 6:5

Are you a person who likes to pray in front of others so you can show them how spiritual you are? Do you try to impress others when you pray? Is it typical for you to rehearse or memorize a prayer if you know you will be praying in front of others? If given the opportunity to pray with others today, do it with a humble spirit.

☐ Pray   ☐ Read   Currently working on _____

Evening Reflection

Day 119

"My son, if sinners entice you, Do not consent."

Proverbs 1:10

Temptation surrounds us, and there is no shortage of people who pull us in the wrong direction. The direction we go is up to us. Today, choose to reject the invitation of temptation.

☐ Pray ☐ Read Currently working on _____

Evening Reflection

Day 120

Mercy Me's song "Bring The Rain" talks about being able to praise the Lord during the storms of life.

Go to www.StumblingServant.com and click on the Morning Thoughts Song Challenges link, then Day 120. There you will find a link to listen to this song. After you listen to the song, determine if you are able to claim it for yourself today.

☐ Pray   ☐ Read   Currently working on _____

Evening Reflection

Day 121

"Let another man praise you, and not your own mouth; A stranger, and not your own lips."

Proverbs 27:2

A person who praises their own name and deeds probably doesn't have anyone else that wants to praise them. Focus on doing your job today, and if someone praises you for it, accept it graciously.

□ Pray   □ Read   Currently working on _____

Evening Reflection

Day 122

"Whoever guards his mouth and tongue
Keeps his soul from troubles."

Proverbs 21:23

Think about all of the extra trouble we have brought on ourselves with the things that we have said. If we really guard the things that we say, we will save ourselves from a lot of unnecessary drama. Act as if the words that you speak today must pass through guards before they come out of your mouth.

☐ Pray   ☐ Read   Currently working on _____

Evening Reflection

Day 123

"Only fear the LORD, and serve Him in truth with all your heart; for consider what great things He has done for you."

1 Samuel 12:24

Think about all the Lord has done for you. Giving up His life for you is enough in itself, but don't take everything else for granted. Truly consider all of the things He has done for you throughout today, and then determine if you are serving Him with all your heart.

☐ Pray   ☐ Read   Currently working on _____

Evening Reflection

Day 124

"Commit your works to the LORD,
And your thoughts will be established."

Proverbs 16:3

If today's challenge is to honor the Lord with all that you do
and you take the challenge seriously, then I would be willing
to bet that at least a few times today you will think about
what you are about to do or what you just did. Commit your
works and see if you don't think about it.

☐ Pray   ☐ Read   Currently working on _____

Evening Reflection

Day 125

"These things also belong to the wise: It is not good to show partiality in judgment."

Proverbs 24:23

Does it ever seem like different people play with different rules? If you are in a position that requires you to discipline people, make sure you do it without partiality. If you're a boss, hold all your employees to the same standards. If you're a teacher, don't allow one student to get away with something others get in trouble for. Hold people, including yourself, accountable today without partiality.

☐ Pray   ☐ Read   Currently working on _____

Evening Reflection

Day 126

"Cease listening to instruction, my son, And you will stray from the words of knowledge."

Proverbs 19:27

Let's pretend you are going fishing alone in the ocean for the first time. You've borrowed your friend's boat and have all the gear you need, including a list of instructions from your friend. You can follow all of the instructions precisely, but if you stop following them before you drop the anchor, sooner or later you will realize that you have drifted from your starting place. Have you quit listening to the instruction of the Lord? If so, you probably have drifted farther than you realize. Take time today to determine if you have drifted because you have quit listening to Christ.

☐ Pray　☐ Read　Currently working on _____

Evening Reflection

Day 127

"As he came from his mother's womb, naked shall he
return, To go as he came; And he shall take nothing from
his labor Which he may carry away in his hand."

Ecclesiastes 5:15

We are all born with no possessions, and we won't be able to
take any of our possessions with us when we die. What we
possess here on earth is of no importance. Focus on Christ
today rather than on your newest purchase or what you want
to buy next.

☐ Pray   ☐ Read   Currently working on _____

Evening Reflection

Day 128

"Incline your ear and hear the words of the wise, And apply your heart to my knowledge;"

Proverbs 22:17

How often do you just sit around and listen? It's easier to offer our opinion than to sit and think about what others are saying. Today, find some wise people that you can listen to.

☐ Pray   ☐ Read   Currently working on _____

Evening Reflection

Day 129

"As iron sharpens iron, So a man sharpens the countenance of his friend."

Proverbs 27:17

Do your friends sharpen or dull your spiritual life? What effect do you have on your friend's spiritual life? When is the last time you talked about something spiritual with your closest friends? I know sometimes I go a long time without discussing anything spiritual with friends. If it has been awhile, then we probably aren't sharpening each other very much. Take time today to talk with a friend about this verse.

SAGE Girls Ministry is teaching young women to sharpen one another. Their mission is to reach, teach, and train young women to impact their communities and the world with the love of Christ. Check out Sage's website: www.SageMinistries.org

☐ Pray   ☐ Read   Currently working on _____

Evening Reflection

Day 130

"Be angry, and do not sin. Meditate within your heart on your bed, and be still. Selah"

Psalm 4:4

It is not a sin to be angry. I would guess that we allow our anger to turn into sin a lot of the time, but it does not have to happen. Rather than lashing back, gossiping, or thinking evil thoughts when you get angry today, take a deep breath and say a prayer.

☐ Pray   ☐ Read   Currently working on _____

Evening Reflection

Day 131

"Go from the presence of a foolish man, When you do not perceive in him the lips of knowledge."

Proverbs 14:7

Instead of hanging around and listening to foolish people talk, we should walk away. It may be entertaining to debate or just listen, but we shouldn't. Today, instead of listening to foolish talk, walk away.

☐ Pray   ☐ Read   Currently working on _____

Evening Reflection

Day 132

"For God so loved the world that He gave His only
begotten Son, that whoever believes in Him should not
perish but have everlasting life."

John 3:16

God loves you so much that He gave His Son as a sacrifice
for you. Be a reflection of that love and sacrifice something
today to help someone else.

☐ Pray ☐ Read Currently working on _____

Evening Reflection

Day 133

"whereas you do not know what will happen tomorrow. For what is your life? It is even a vapor that appears for a little time and then vanishes away."

James 4:14

Your life will vanish before you know it. Are you making an impact that will last after you are gone? A few summers ago, I went to Kenya with Vapor International. Today, take time to visit this website and learn more about what they are doing. www.VaporInternational.org

□ Pray   □ Read   Currently working on _____

Evening Reflection

Day 134

"Oh come, let us worship and bow down; Let us kneel before the Lord our Maker."

Psalm 95:6

Kneeling down is a sign of submissiveness. Submitting is a sign of weakness in today's society. As Christians, we will never be the best we can be unless we submit everything to Christ. How often do you kneel down in submission before your Savior? Do it today, tomorrow, and the next day......

☐ Pray   ☐ Read   Currently working on _____

Evening Reflection

Day 135

Matt Redman's song "The Heart of Worship" is something I believe we should reflect on consistently.

Go to www.StumblingServant.com and click on the Morning Thoughts Song Challenges link, then Day 135. There you will find a link to listen to this song. Make sure your worship is all about Him and only about Him today.

☐ Pray   ☐ Read   Currently working on _____

Evening Reflection

Day 136

"For judgment is without mercy to the one who has shown
no mercy. Mercy triumphs over judgment."

James 2:13

If you are found guilty of a crime, the judge can still have
mercy on you. Most of the time the amount of mercy we
receive is based on our history. If we would like people to
have mercy on us when we mess up, then we must also show
others mercy when they mess up. Be a person of mercy
today.

☐ Pray   ☐ Read   Currently working on _____

Evening Reflection

153

Day 137

"Wisdom calls aloud outside; She raises her voice
in the open squares."

Proverbs 1:20

Wisdom wants to be found. She isn't hidden; she is accessible.
Have you been listening for her? Today, as you go about your
day, seek after wisdom.

☐ Pray   ☐ Read   Currently working on _____

Evening Reflection

Day 138

"but grow in the grace and knowledge of our Lord
and Savior Jesus Christ…"

2nd Peter 3:18

If something is not growing, then it is dying. Have you been
growing in your knowledge of Christ? How gracious of a
person are you? Today, seek to grow in both of these areas.

☐ Pray   ☐ Read   Currently working on _____

Evening Reflection

Day 139

"Debate your case with your neighbor,
And do not disclose the secret to another;"

Proverbs 25:9

We have all talked about someone behind their back at one point or another, but some people thrive on it. We all know someone who likes to talk about other people. A common saying goes, "If you don't know of anyone that likes doing it, then you may be the one others are thinking of." If you have a problem with someone, make a point today not to discuss it with other people.

☐ Pray ☐ Read Currently working on _____

Evening Reflection

Day 140

How often do you see a car that looks like a car that belongs to someone you know? I'm sure I'm not the only one that tries to catch a glimpse of the person driving to see if it is the person I know or not. If it turns out to be that person, we try to get their attention and wave, but if not, we go about our way. From now on when you see a car that reminds you of someone you know, take a minute to pray for them regardless of who the driver of the car may be.

☐ Pray   ☐ Read   Currently working on _____

Evening Reflection

Day 141

"Be hospitable to one another without grumbling."

1 Peter 4:9

Have you ever done something for someone else with a smile on your face and then complained about it when you were no longer in their presence? I know I have. Don't allow yourself to complain today.

☐ Pray   ☐ Read   Currently working on _____

Evening Reflection

Day 142

"Finally, my brethren, be strong in the Lord and in the power of His might. Put on the whole armor of God, that you may be able to stand against the wiles of the devil. For we do not wrestle against flesh and blood, but against principalities, against powers, against the rulers of the darkness of this age, against spiritual hosts of wickedness in the heavenly places. Therefore take up the whole armor of God, that you may be able to withstand in the evil day, and having done all, to stand….and having shod your feet with the preparation of the gospel of peace;"

Ephesians 6:10-13,15

Today is focusing on another aspect of the armor of God. No matter what battles come our way, we need to have peace. It is also important for us to maintain peace by avoiding petty drama and conflict. There is a time to stand our ground, but some of the time we choose to stand our ground over what is ultimately meaningless. Today, have peace that the Lord is with you whatever comes your way, and choose to walk the path of peace when faced with insignificant conflict.

☐ Pray ☐ Read Currently working on _____

Evening Reflection

Day 143

"He who disdains instruction despises his own soul, But he who heeds rebuke gets understanding."

Proverbs 15:32

He who listens to disapproval gains understanding. How many of us like to listen to someone who disapproves of what we are doing? I know I don't. No matter what you do, someone is likely to disapprove of it. My dad once told me, "No matter what you do, there will always be people who like you and people who don't like you." We must make sure we listen to those people who have our best interest at heart, even if they disapprove of something we are doing. Be willing to take constructive criticism today.

☐ Pray   ☐ Read   Currently working on _____

Evening Reflection

Day 144

"'Naked I came from my mother's womb, And naked shall I return there. The LORD gave, and the LORD has taken away; Blessed be the name of the LORD.' In all this Job did not sin nor charge God with wrong."

Job 1:21-22

Job was given a lot, but he also lost a lot. He realized that he was born with nothing and would take nothing with him when he died. In the midst of his tragedy, he was able to see the big picture. Often, we let the smallest things distract us from the big picture. We get cut off on the way to work or someone bumps into us in the hallway at school and we are angry the rest of our day. Don't allow anything to shift your focus from Christ today.

☐ Pray   ☐ Read   Currently working on _____

Evening Reflection

Day 145

"My son, if your heart is wise, My heart will rejoice—
indeed, I myself;"

Proverbs 23:15

If our earthly Fathers rejoice when we are wise, then how
much more does our Heavenly Father rejoice? Take a minute
to think about that. The God who created the earth, the God
who constructed the universe, the God whose very breath
we breathe rejoices when we are wise. There are not many
things more amazing than that. Be wise and cause the Lord
to rejoice today.

☐ Pray   ☐ Read   Currently working on _____

Evening Reflection

Day 146

"And do not be conformed to this world, but be transformed by the renewing of your mind, that you may prove what is that good and acceptable and perfect will of God."

Romans 12:2

I often hear people say, "We don't need to be doing the things the world is doing." While that is true, it seems that doing things the world is *not* doing gets overlooked. It's not good enough to not do the things we shouldn't, without doing the things we should. "Be transformed by the renewing" tells us that something has to happen more than once. If you just do something once, then you aren't renewing it. Becoming more like Christ is not a one time circumstance, it's a daily action. Each day we are given hundreds, if not thousands, of choices that will either bring us closer to Christ or further from Him. Pray and ask God to help your mind focus on Him throughout today.

☐ Pray   ☐ Read   Currently working on _____

Evening Reflection

Day 147

"And suddenly a great tempest arose on the sea, so that the boat was covered with the waves. But He was asleep. Then His disciples came to Him and awoke Him, saying, 'Lord, save us! We are perishing!' But He said to them, 'Why are you fearful, O you of little faith?' Then He arose and rebuked the winds and the sea, and there was a great calm."

Matthew 8:24-26

Do the storms of life have you fearful? Maybe it's the potential loss of a job. Maybe someone has done something to you that you have not told anyone else about. Maybe you or someone you love is battling an illness. Maybe a family member or friend is going astray. Maybe you have an addiction no one else knows about. Maybe you feel pressure from those around you to be something you don't want to be. Maybe you have a weakness that you just can't seem to overcome. We all deal with storms. Some are real storms like hurricanes and tornadoes, but others don't involve the weather at all. The disciples were on the same boat with Christ, yet they were afraid they would die. Those of us that have a relationship with Christ can consider ourselves as being on the same boat with Christ. No matter how bad the storm may be, Jesus will never jump ship. Be sure that Jesus is the captain of your ship today and not just a deckhand.

☐ Pray   ☐ Read   Currently working on _____

Evening Reflection

Day 148

"Therefore by their fruits you will know them."

Matthew 7:20

What have your actions been producing? Can others look at what you have done and tell that you are a Christian? Reflect on the results you have been producing today, and see what they tell others about you.

☐ Pray ☐ Read Currently working on _____

Evening Reflection

166

Day 149

"For whoever does the will of God is My brother and
My sister and mother."

Mark 3:35

"Does" implies action. Is there action in your relationship
with God? Today, do what you know He wants you to do.

☐ Pray   ☐ Read   Currently working on _____

Evening Reflection

Day 150

Casting Crowns' song "If We are the Body" asks questions that we as Christians need to answer.

Go to www.StumblingServant.com and click on the Morning Thoughts Song Challenges link, then Day 150. There you will find links to read the lyrics of this song and to listen to it. After doing so, think about the questions the song asks throughout today.

☐ Pray   ☐ Read   Currently working on _____

Evening Reflection

Day 151

"By pride comes nothing but strife, But with the
well-advised is wisdom."

Proverbs 13:10

Strife, conflict, drama, controversy. Who wakes up in the
morning looking forward to any of those things? There are
times that they can not be avoided, but the majority of the
time they are a result of pride. We don't like to admit we
are wrong, don't want to take the time to listen to someone
else, form our opinion before we know all the facts, or think
our way is the only way to do something. Life is a lot more
relaxing without any of the petty conflicts. Swallow your
pride and avoid the meaningless conflict you could engage
in today, even if you are right.

☐ Pray   ☐ Read   Currently working on _____

Evening Reflection

Day 152

"casting all your care upon Him, for He cares for you."

1 Peter 5:7

Have you given all of your concerns to the Lord? How much thought have you put into the fact that the Creator of the universe cares for you? That is amazing. Today, begin the process of casting all of your cares upon Him instead of trying to solve them by yourself.

☐ Pray   ☐ Read   Currently working on _____

Evening Reflection

Day 153

"By this all will know that you are My disciples,
if you have love for one another."

John 13:35

Can you be identified as a follower of Christ because of your love for others? In your own way, take time today to show Christ's love to someone else.

☐ Pray ☐ Read Currently working on _____

Evening Reflection

Day 154

"Enter into His gates with thanksgiving,
And into His courts with praise. Be thankful to Him,
and bless His name."

Psalm 100:4

Too often we complain and question God rather than thank and praise Him. Sometimes when something does not go the way I would like it to, I allow that one thing to affect my attitude more than all the things He has blessed me with. We have to keep the big picture in mind. We are all blessed beyond anything we deserve. Thank the Lord and praise Him today for all the things you have and don't deserve.

☐ Pray   ☐ Read   Currently working on _____

Evening Reflection

Day 155

"Do not say, 'I will recompense evil'; Wait for the Lord, and He will save you."

Proverbs 20:22

It is human nature to want to get even with someone who has done us wrong or to try to settle the score ourselves, but God commands us not to. To me, this is one of the hardest aspects of self-control. Today, evaluate your willingness to wait on the Lord.

☐ Pray   ☐ Read   Currently working on _____

Evening Reflection

Day 156

"Do not lust after her beauty in your heart, Nor let her allure you with her eyelids."

Proverbs 6:25

This verse is in a passage talking about adultery. It talks about lusting after beauty, but we can lust over someone for other reasons as well. You can lust for someone because of their wealth, intelligence, job status, possessions, and many other traits. Are you lusting after someone else? It is wrong, regardless of if you are married or not. Deny yourself from lusting after anyone or anything today.

☐ Pray   ☐ Read   Currently working on _____

Evening Reflection

Day 157

"The beginning of strife is like releasing water; Therefore stop contention before a quarrel starts."

Proverbs 17:14

Once water breaks through an object, it is very hard and messy to get the leak plugged. Is there a relationship in your life that is about to spring a leak? Maybe things are uneasy with a parent, sibling, friend, spouse, or coworker. Make today the first day in the process of preventing a messy situation.

☐ Pray   ☐ Read   Currently working on _____

Evening Reflection

Day 158

"As in water face reflects face,
So a man's heart reveals the man"

Proverbs 27:19

Wouldn't it be great if we could look inside and see how much our heart reflects Christ? Although it would be cool, we don't need to do that. Our actions reflect our heart. You may be thinking, "Hold on, my heart is better than I act," and sometimes I use that argument as well, but in reality it isn't. If our actions (a) reflect Christ (C), then our heart (h) will reflect Christ (C) also. Make sure today that a=C.

☐ Pray   ☐ Read   Currently working on _____

Evening Reflection

Day 159

"Better is a little with righteousness,
Than vast revenues without justice."

Proverbs 16:8

($1 + righteousness) > ($1,000,000 – justice)

Is this a formula you agree with? If given a chance to have either combination, which one would you take? I would like to think I would take the first pair, but I would probably take the money and try to buy justice. Today, focus on becoming more concerned with becoming righteous than becoming rich.

☐ Pray   ☐ Read   Currently working on _____

Evening Reflection

Day 160

"Confess your trespasses to one another, and pray for one another, that you may be healed. The effective, fervent prayer of a righteous man avails much."

James 5:16

Do you have friends that you can talk about your struggles with? Do you have friends you can pray with? Do you have friends you can ask to pray for you and be confident they will do so? Are you a friend others can come to when they need to talk about their struggles? Do others ask you to pray for them? Determine today if you have friends like this and if you are this type of friend.

☐ Pray   ☐ Read   Currently working on _____

Evening Reflection

Day 161

"And why do you look at the speck in your brother's eye,
but do not consider the plank in your own eye?"

Matthew 7:3

It is much easier to talk about what is wrong with other
people than to address what is wrong with ourselves. We
all have weaknesses. We all have done things we wish we
would not have done. None of us are perfect. Rather than
inspecting others to see what is wrong with them, evaluate
yourself today and find things you need to improve.

☐ Pray   ☐ Read   Currently working on _____

Evening Reflection

Day 162

"For as we have many members in one body, but all the members do not have the same function, so we, being many, are one body in Christ, and individually members of one another."

Romans 12:4-5

If we as believers are one body, why is it so hard to work together? No, everyone does not believe the same thing, but for those of us that do, aren't we on the same team? The easiest way to bring a team down is from within. Work with your fellow believers in Christ today.

☐ Pray ☐ Read Currently working on _____

Evening Reflection

Day 163

"My son, give me your heart,
And let your eyes observe my ways."

Proverbs 23:26

What are your eyes focused on? Being popular at school, the job promotion, a new car, the gift you want for Christmas or your birthday, your bank account, the number of people that attend your church services, your looks, a new house, or on Christ? If we are going to observe the ways of Christ, then we can't be focused on ourselves. If we are going to imitate the actions of Christ, then we will put God first and others second. Pray and ask the Lord to help you see things through His eyes today.

☐ Pray ☐ Read Currently working on _____

Evening Reflection

Day 164

"And David said, 'What have I done now?
Is there not a cause?'"

1 Samuel 17:29

When the rest of the Israelites were in fear of Goliath, David wasn't. He began to ask those around him if there was not reason to face the giant. He did not let the fear and the lack of faith of those around him drag him down. He knew that His God was mightier than the giant. Are you allowing the fear or the lack of faith of others drag you down? Has the Lord put something on your heart that you have shared with others, only to be discouraged by their response? If He has put something on your heart, is there not a cause? He can use you just like He used David. Take a step today in doing what the Lord has put on your heart.

☐ Pray   ☐ Read   Currently working on _____

Evening Reflection

Day 165

Brandon Heath's song "Give Me Your Eyes" is a request for the Lord to allow us to see people as He sees them.

Go to www.StumblingServant.com and click on the Morning Thoughts Song Challenges link, then Day 165. There you will find links to read the lyrics of this song, to listen to it, and to watch the music video for it. After doing so, ask the Lord to help you see people through His eyes today. We will never see the needs of others if our heads are hanging down or if our noses are up in the air. Be humbly confident.

☐ Pray   ☐ Read   Currently working on _____

Evening Reflection

Day 166

"But Peter and the other apostles answered and said: 'We ought to obey God rather than men.'"

Acts 5:29

This was the apostles' reply to the captain of the temple and the officers who had commanded them to stop teaching about Jesus. They said this to people who had already thrown them in jail. Would you be that bold, or do you have room to grow like me? Ask God to prepare you today for what you will go through tomorrow, and then do your part.

☐ Pray ☐ Read Currently working on _____

Evening Reflection

Day 167

"Do not let your heart envy sinners, But be zealous for the fear of the Lord all the day;"

Proverbs 23:17

Sometimes it seems like the people who do things the wrong way are always coming out on top. This verse tells us not to envy them, but instead continue living in respect of our Lord. Today, focus on how you can better serve your Lord rather than on what those around you are doing.

☐ Pray　☐ Read　Currently working on _____

Evening Reflection

Day 168

I'm not sure about the rest of the country, but here in Texas roadside crosses that mark the place where someone lost their life are a common sight. When you drive past a roadside cross, be in prayer for that person's family and friends. Pray that if they do not have a relationship with Christ, that they would begin one. Also pray for comfort, peace, support from those close to them, and that the Lord would bring good from the situation. Remember, a roadside cross doesn't just signify the death of a person, it also signifies family and friends that are living with the loss of a loved one.

☐ Pray ☐ Read   Currently working on _____

Evening Reflection

Day 169

"'For My thoughts are not your thoughts, Nor are your ways My ways,' says the LORD. 'For as the heavens are higher than the earth, So are My ways higher than your ways, And My thoughts than your thoughts.'"

Isaiah 55:8-9

Are you content thinking your thoughts and doing things your way? Do you desire to think as God thinks and to do things the way He wants them done? Do you pray that the things you are doing or planning on doing will fail if they are not what the Lord wants you to do? Pray that your ways fail today.

☐ Pray ☐ Read Currently working on _____

Evening Reflection

Day 170

"A wrathful man stirs up strife, But he who is slow
to anger allays contention."

Proverbs 15:18

Are you a person who brings a sense of calm to controversy
or a person who likes to stir things up? When something
happens to you, do your actions calm those around you, or
do they encourage foolish action? Work on being a calming
presence today.

☐ Pray   ☐ Read   Currently working on _____

Evening Reflection

Day 171

"Better is a dinner of herbs where love is,
Than a fatted calf with hatred."

Proverbs 15:17

Peas (insert one of your least favorite foods) + love > steak (insert one of your favorite foods) + hatred.

No matter what it is you may eat today, have a sprit of love towards those present.

☐ Pray   ☐ Read   Currently working on _____

Evening Reflection

Day 172

"'You have put all things in subjection under his feet.' For in that He put all in subjection under him, He left nothing that is not put under him. But now we do not yet see all things put under him."

Hebrews 2:8

The Lord trusts you with everything He created. Do other people trust you to get something done? Would they trust you to take care of their most precious possession? The Lord trusts us with more than we even realize. The Lord has given us the responsibility of telling others about Him. What would your grade look like if the Lord graded you on telling others about Him? Regardless of how your grade would look, today is a new day. Live today like the Lord is depending on you to carry out His work, because He is.

☐ Pray   ☐ Read   Currently working on ＿＿＿＿＿＿

Evening Reflection

Day 173

"Restore to me the joy of Your salvation, And uphold me by Your generous Spirit."

Psalm 51:12

Have you lost some of the joy you once had for your Savior? Today, think back on when your relationship with Christ began, and determine if you have lost some of the joy.

☐ Pray   ☐ Read   Currently working on _____

Evening Reflection

Day 174

"Oh, give thanks to the LORD! Call upon His name;
Make known His deeds among the peoples!"

1 Chronicles 16:8

How often do you tell others of the good things the Lord
has done for you--not out of pride, but giving Him glory
for what He has done? It seems like we are always willing to
share prayer requests with friends, but I hardly ever hear or
share any praises. Take time today to share something the
Lord has done for you with others.

☐ Pray ☐ Read Currently working on _____

Evening Reflection

Day 175

"And she brought forth her firstborn Son, and wrapped
Him in swaddling cloths, and laid Him in a manger,
because there was no room for them in the inn."

Luke 2:7

The Creator of the tree that was used to make this paper, the
Creator of the material that was used to make the clothes you
are wearing, the Creator of the food that you will eat today,
the Creator of everything that has ever existed, was laid in a
manger after His birth. Mary didn't put Him in a onesie that
said "I Rock," she wrapped Him in a sheet. If any of us were
given the opportunity to pick how our birth would play out,
how many of us would have picked this? I know I wouldn't
have. God in the form of man, Jesus, slept in a manger. If
that doesn't make us question some of the things we think we
deserve, nothing will. Today, think about the level of luxury
Jesus had and the things He owned, and compare it to what
you think you need.

☐ Pray   ☐ Read   Currently working on _____

Evening Reflection

Day 176

"For as the body without the spirit is dead, so faith without works is dead also."

James 2:26

We can't work our way into Heaven, but if our faith doesn't compel us to serve Christ and to do things for others, then we probably don't have true faith. Let your actions show that you love Christ today.

☐ Pray   ☐ Read   Currently working on _____

Evening Reflection

Day 177

"For with God nothing will be impossible."

Luke 1:37

This is another verse we like to claim during the difficult times of life. God made the impossible happen for Elizabeth, the mother of John the Baptist. Elizabeth was not able to have children. She and her husband Zacharias were also very old. Lets look at verse 6 from the same chapter. It says, "And they were both righteous before God, walking in all the commandments and ordinances of the Lord blameless." Having John was not impossible because they were walking with God. If we want to claim this verse, we must walk with God. We can't neglect our part and expect Him to do everything. Walk with God today, and let Him accomplish the impossible.

☐ Pray   ☐ Read   Currently working on _____

Evening Reflection

Day 178

"The stone which the builders rejected Has become the chief cornerstone."

Psalm 118:22

Have you ever felt rejected? Odds are, if you are truly trying to live like Christ, you know what rejection feels like. Maybe it's from your friends for not going to the parties. It could be from walking away from others at work when they start to talk about someone else. Maybe the Lord put something on your heart that others didn't think was a good idea. Jesus Himself was rejected. Seek after Christ no matter who may reject you today.

☐ Pray   ☐ Read   Currently working on _____

Evening Reflection

Day 179

"Hear, my son, and be wise;
And guide your heart in the way."

Proverbs 23:19

If you are talking, you aren't listening. If you aren't listening,
you aren't learning from anyone else. If you aren't learning
from anyone else, you are learning from yourself. If you are
learning from yourself, you are wise in your own eyes. Today,
don't just listen--*hear*.

☐ Pray   ☐ Read   Currently working on _____

Evening Reflection

Day 180

Matthew West's song "My Own Little World" sums up how a lot of us Christians are living these days.

Go to www.StumblingServant.com and click on the Morning Thoughts Song Challenges link, then Day 180. There you will find links to read the lyrics to this song, to listen to it, and to watch the official music video for it. Evaluate your life today and determine if you're living for the wrong things.

☐ Pray   ☐ Read   Currently working on _____

Evening Reflection

Day 181

"Better to be of a humble spirit with the lowly, Than to divide the spoil with the proud."

Proverbs 16:19

Would you rather hang out with the humble people at the bottom of the totem pole or the proud people calling the shots? What percentage of the people calling the shots do you think would be willing to clean the toilets? Of course, it all depends on the person, but I would guess it's a pretty small percentage. Offer a hand to someone performing a task that our society considers "lowly" today.

☐ Pray   ☐ Read   Currently working on _____

Evening Reflection

Day 182

"There are many plans in a man's heart, Nevertheless the LORD's counsel—that will stand."

Proverbs 19:21

Plans are something that most people have. Some of them are good, but others are not. Some are brief, while others are detailed. Even when we have the best of intentions, our plans may not be in line with the Lord's. He has a purpose for our life, and it is up to us to fulfill it. Spend time today praying for God's plans to guide your life, not your own.

☐ Pray   ☐ Read   Currently working on _____

Evening Reflection

Day 183

"Because the foolishness of God is wiser than men, and the weakness of God is stronger than men."

1 Corinthians 1:25

No matter how wise or powerful you have become, or will become, it does not compare to God. Comparing our wisdom and strength to God's is like a drop of rain compared to the rest of water on Earth combined. Even the biggest raindrop doesn't compare. Today, view yourself as a drop of rain in the ocean of God.

☐ Pray ☐ Read Currently working on _____

Evening Reflection

Day 184

"Jesus Wept."

John 11:35

Is there something you are upset about? Has something brought you to tears lately? Remember that Jesus knows your pain. Even the Savior of the world shed tears. He not only knows everything you are going through, but He can relate to you because He walked this earth Himself. The Lord is wiser than anyone you know. He cares more about you than anyone ever could. His Word offers answers to all of life's issues. Today, be confident the Lord understands your tears because He shed them Himself. Has it been a long time since you have cried? Do you feel that your heart has grown cold? If so, ask the Lord to begin softening your heart today.

☐ Pray   ☐ Read   Currently working on _____

Evening Reflection

Day 185

"Their land is also full of idols; They worship the work of their own hands, That which their own fingers have made."

Isaiah 2:8

I believe this is a problem we face as Christians. You may be thinking, "You are crazy; I don't bow down to statues." Well, I don't either, but how much time and energy do we put into attaining earthly treasures? I don't believe it is wrong to have nice things, but it becomes a problem when we put more time into attaining possessions than the time we put into our relationships with Christ and those He has placed in our life. Keep a log of the way you spend your time today, and reflect on it tonight.

☐ Pray   ☐ Read   Currently working on _____

Evening Reflection

Day 186

"All the ways of a man are pure in his own eyes, But the LORD weighs the spirits."

Proverbs 16:2

How many of us are totally honest with ourselves about why we do what we do? Do we go to church because it is time to go or because we truly want to hear a message from the Lord? Do we sing because we sound good or because we want to worship our Savior? Do we want our churches to grow so we have more numbers or so we can equip more people to serve our communities? We can fool others most of the time, and can even fool ourselves some of the time, but we can never fool God. Ask Him to reveal to you something in your spirit that you are blind to today.

☐ Pray   ☐ Read   Currently working on _____

Evening Reflection

Day 187

"If any of you lacks wisdom, let him ask of God,
who gives to all liberally and without reproach,
and it will be given to him."

James 1:5

Do you lack wisdom? I sure know I do. Knowing you lack wisdom is the first step to gaining wisdom. This verse tells us that if we ask God for wisdom, He will give it to us. Today, ask God to give you wisdom, and then seek after it.

☐ Pray   ☐ Read   Currently working on _____

Evening Reflection

Day 188

"It is better to hear the rebuke of the wise Than for a man to hear the song of fools."

Ecclesiastes 7:5

How many of us would choose rebuke over entertainment? I know I wouldn't. This tells us how valuable it is to have wise people in our lives. Have you ever asked someone you consider to be wise what areas they think you should work on? Today, embrace the correction of the wise rather than being offended by it.

☐ Pray   ☐ Read   Currently working on _____

Evening Reflection

Day 189

"But you, when you pray, go into your room, and when
you have shut your door, pray to your Father who is in the
secret place; and your father who sees in secret will
reward you openly."

Matthew 6:6

Somehow I don't think Jesus was telling us to pray in secret
for what we want to be rewarded with in the open. Pray in
secret today, and don't ask for anything.

☐ Pray   ☐ Read   Currently working on _____

Evening Reflection

Day 190

"But be doers of the word, and not hearers only,
deceiving yourselves."

James 1:22

I question how many of us are even hearers of the Word.
After we pick and choose what parts of the Bible we want
to hear, we argue about what it means. Meanwhile, we are
accomplishing nothing. Are you truly a hearer of the Word?
If so, then do something it tells you to do today.

☐ Pray   ☐ Read   Currently working on _____

Evening Reflection

Day 191

"to speak evil of no one, to be peaceable, gentle, showing all humility to all men."

Titus 3:2

Do you talk about others? Are you a peaceful person? Are you a gentle person? Are you a humble person? Can you be a peaceful person and talk about others? Can you be a humble person and not treat others gently? Take time to evaluate yourself in these areas today.

☐ Pray   ☐ Read   Currently working on _____

Evening Reflection

Day 192

"Only let your conduct be worthy of the gospel of Christ, so that whether I come and see you or am absent, I may hear of your affairs, that you stand fast in one spirit, with one mind striving together for the faith of the gospel,"

Philippians 1:27

Is your conduct worthy of the price Christ paid for you? I know mine isn't all the time. How much would our world change if all believers lived this out? Let your conduct today show that you are thankful for the sacrifice Christ made for you.

☐ Pray   ☐ Read   Currently working on _____

Evening Reflection

Day 193

"Hell and Destruction are never full; So the eyes of
man are never satisfied."

Proverbs 27:20

As humans we will always want the next best thing. We will
get a new car, and then a new model will be released that we
will want the next year. We will buy a house and then see a
feature in another person's house and want to add it to ours.
We will go on vacation to a part of the country we have never
been then see pictures of someone's vacation overseas and
want to go there. The sooner we realize that no matter what
we get, there will always be something else we would like to
have, the better. Be thankful today for the things God has
given you, and take care of them as if they were the newest
thing out.

☐ Pray   ☐ Read   Currently working on _____

Evening Reflection

Day 194

"Remember the days of old, Consider the years of many generations. Ask your father, and he will show you; Your elders, and they will tell you:"

Deuteronomy 32:7

How often do we sit down and listen to the stories of our elders? There is so much wisdom that we do not take advantage of because we think we have everything figured out or that things aren't the same today as they were back in their day. We should be like a sponge soaking up all of their knowledge and wisdom. Seek out an elder today and ask for advice on life.

☐ Pray   ☐ Read   Currently working on _____

Evening Reflection

Day 195

Switchfoot's song "This is Your Life" asks about the person we have become.

Go to www.StumblingServant.com and click on the Morning Thoughts Song Challenges link, then Day 195. There you will find a link to read the lyrics to this song and another link to listen to it. After you read the lyrics or listen to the song, determine if your life is what you want it to be. Is what you want it to be what God wants it to be? Think about those two questions today.

☐ Pray ☐ Read Currently working on _____

Evening Reflection

Day 196

Monthly Prayer

What do you do when you are getting close to a traffic light and it turns yellow? I know what I do. Most of the time I hit the gas. It doesn't matter if I am running late or if I am just on my way home; I don't want to be stuck at a red light. It seems that we believe that sitting still is an inconvenience. We always have to be on the move or have something to occupy our attention. Why are we constantly in a rush, even when we aren't pressed for time? From now on, don't hit the gas when you see a yellow light all the time. Slow down, sit through the red light, and take in the sights around you that God created. Observe His creations and thank Him for the things that you see. Praise Him for giving you another day.

☐ Pray   ☐ Read   Currently working on _____

Evening Reflection

Day 197

"If you really fulfill the royal law according to the
Scripture, 'You shall love your neighbor as yourself,'
you do well."

James 2:8

How "well" have you been doing? How do you treat those
you come into contact with on a daily basis? Do you value
others as much as you do yourself? Are you concerned about
the hard times of others as much as your own? Evaluate your
level of love for others today.

☐ Pray   ☐ Read   Currently working on _____

Evening Reflection

Day 198

"Philip said to Him, 'Lord, show us the Father,
and it is sufficient for us.'"

John 14:8

Philip asked Jesus to show them the Father. In this passage
Jesus explains that He and the Father are one. How many
times do we know what God wants us to do, but we still ask
for more assurance? We pray for something, He opens the
door, and then we say, "Show me that wasn't a coincidence
by…" Today, when the Lord puts something on your heart,
don't ask for a sign, follow His lead!

☐ Pray   ☐ Read   Currently working on _____

Evening Reflection

Day 199

"Through the Lord's mercies we are not consumed,
Because His compassions fail not. They are new every
morning; Great is Your faithfulness."

Lamentations 3:22-23

God's mercy is new every day. Whatever may have happened
yesterday, last week, or 5 years ago can't be changed. Learn
from the failures of the past and focus on today. Today, claim
victory over the things in your past, and do not allow them
to bring you down any longer.

☐ Pray   ☐ Read   Currently working on _____

Evening Reflection

Day 200

"The refining pot is for silver and the furnace for gold,
And a man is valued by what others say of him."

Proverbs 27:21

What do others say about you? Not those who don't care for
you or those who tell you what you want to hear, but those
who care and will call it like they see it. Do you already have
people like this you can go talk to? If not, think about the
people you know and see if any of them fit that mold. If so,
then take time today to ask them about your strengths and
weaknesses.

☐ Pray   ☐ Read   Currently working on _____

Evening Reflection

Day 201

"For if there should come into your assembly a man with gold rings, in fine apparel, and there should also come in a poor man in filthy clothes, and you pay attention to the one wearing the fine clothes and say to him, "You sit here in a good place," and say to the poor man, "You stand there," or, "Sit here at my footstool," have you not shown partiality among yourselves, and become judges with evil thoughts?"

James 2:2-4

If a man dressed in a fancy suit and a man dressed in dirty clothes were to enter a restaurant at the same time, who would be seated first? If the same two men were to approach you on on the street at separate times, who would you be more likely to stop and talk to? If you saw both men needed help picking up books they dropped, who would you be more likely to help? Don't cater to others based on the way they look today.

☐ Pray   ☐ Read   Currently working on _____

Evening Reflection

219

Day 202

"I went by the field of the lazy man, And by the vineyard of the man devoid of understanding; And there it was, all overgrown with thorns; Its surface was covered with nettles; Its stone wall was broken down."

Proverbs 24:30-31

Obviously a field or vineyard in this condition is not much good. Maybe today you feel like you are being overtaken with the thorns in your life. The good news is, with some hard landscaping work, things can get back to where they should be. No matter where we are in our lives, we always have something we can weed out or cut down. Make today the first day of getting rid of the overgrown weeds in your life.

☐ Pray   ☐ Read   Currently working on _____

Evening Reflection

Day 203

"for it is not you who speak, but the Spirit of your
Father who speaks in you."

Matthew 10:20

This verse is in a passage where Jesus is talking to the
disciples about being brought before leaders concerning
their faith, but this applies to us today as well. At one
point or another, we have all neglected to talk to someone
about Christ because we think, "I don't know what to
say." Today, ask God to help you see who He brings into
your life to talk with about Him, and then allow Him
to speak through you.

☐ Pray   ☐ Read   Currently working on _____

Evening Reflection

Day 204

"Pure and undefiled religion before God and the Father is this: to visit orphans and widows in their trouble, and to keep oneself unspotted from the world."

James 1:27

When was the last time you spent time with orphans or widows? You may be thinking, "I don't know any orphans or widows." Every nursing home has some widows or widowers. I'm sure they have some who never get a visit from family members. Our society is full of orphans. We have kids whose parents have died, some kids who have been abandoned, and others who live with their parents but have no relationship with them. You are just the right age to show the love of Christ to someone who desperately needs it. Pray for the Lord to show you that person today.

☐ Pray   ☐ Read   Currently working on _____

Evening Reflection
_____
_____
_____
_____
_____
_____
_____
_____
_____

Day 205

"But while he thought about these things, behold,
an angel of the Lord appeared to him in a dream, saying,
'Joseph, son of David, do not be afraid to take to you
Mary your wife, for that which is conceived in
her is of the Holy Spirit.'"

Matthew 1:20

"While he thought." How many of us guys would sit and think about things if our fiancé told us she was pregnant and we knew it wasn't ours? My only thoughts would have been, "What can I use this honeymoon money on?" and "How much can I sell that ring for?" Joseph displays some incredible wisdom here. When given the opportunity to rush into action today, take time to think like Joseph did.

☐ Pray   ☐ Read   Currently working on _____

Evening Reflection

Day 206

"Wash yourselves, make yourselves clean; Put away the evil of your doings from before My eyes. Cease to do evil, Learn to do good; Seek justice, Rebuke the oppressor; Defend the fatherless, Plead for the widow."

Isaiah 1:16-17

There is a lot in this verse, but let's focus on our need to stop doing evil and learning to do good. Doing good isn't natural; it is something we must work at. If you see someone being made fun of or disrespected today, stand up for them peacefully. If you know a child that does not have a father, take some time out of your day to do something for them. If you know someone who has lost their husband or wife, let them know you are thinking about and praying for them. Ask the Lord to give you someone to do something good for today.

☐ Pray   ☐ Read   Currently working on _____

Evening Reflection

Day 207

"Husbands, love your wives, just as Christ also loved the church and gave Himself for her,"

Ephesians 5:25

———————————

"Therefore, just as the church is subject to Christ, so let the wives be to their own husbands in everything."

Ephesians 5:24

———————————

"Children, obey your parents in the Lord, for this is right. 'Honor your father and mother,' which is the first commandment with promise: 'that it may be well with you and you may live long on the earth.'"

Ephesians 6:1-3

Husbands - How does the love that you show your wife compare to the love that Christ showed the church? Obviously He died for the church, and if you are reading this, you haven't died for your wife. What about putting her before yourself? Do you insist on doing what you want to do all the time, or do you do things she enjoys as well? Reflect on this today. Make plans to show your wife you love her in the near future (on a day other than a holiday, birthday, or anniversary) by doing something you know she enjoys.

Wives – Is your husband the head of the house? Do you support him even if you think he is making a bad decision (that doesn't put you or your family in danger)? Do you have faith in him to lead you in the right direction? Does he have the confidence that you support him? Take time to show him you support him sometime other than a holiday, birthday, or anniversary.

Children – Do you obey your parents? We are not supposed to obey our parents because they say so, but because the Lord says so. Unless we are instructed to do something that is sin, we as children are obligated to obey our parents regardless of their faith. Obey your parents today because it is the right thing to do.

☐ Pray   ☐ Read   Currently working on _____

Evening Reflection

Day 208

"Therefore you are inexcusable, O man, whoever you are who judge, for in whatever you judge another you condemn yourself; for you who judge practice the same things."

Romans 2:1

Why is it so easy to judge others? This verse tells us that there is no excuse to do so. Not only is there no excuse, but when we judge others, we automatically condemn ourselves. Avoid condemning yourself by refusing to judge others today.

☐ Pray   ☐ Read   Currently working on _____

Evening Reflection

Day 209

"The heart of the wise teaches his mouth, And adds learning to his lips."

Proverbs 16:23

Is your heart teaching your mouth, or is it feeling bad for what has come out of your mouth? Have your lips learned anything from the times you have put your foot in your mouth? Think back to some foolish things you have said and reflect on what you have learned today.

☐ Pray   ☐ Read   Currently working on _____

Evening Reflection

Day 210

The Sidewalk Prophets' song "The Words I Would Say" is about what they would tell a hurting friend.

Go to www.StumblingServant.com and click on the Morning Thoughts Song Challenges link, then Day 210. There you will find links to read the lyrics to this song, to listen to it, and to watch a video of the song. Today, remember that if you have a relationship with the Lord, He has his hand on you. Don't be afraid or give up. If you have a friend who is hurting reach out to them today.

☐ Pray ☐ Read Currently working on _____

Evening Reflection

Day 211

"Most men will proclaim each his own goodness,
But who can find a faithful man?"

Proverbs 20:6

How much do you talk about yourself? Do you like to flaunt
your accomplishments? Do you have a title that you insist
that other's use? When tempted to brag about yourself today,
remember that you are filthy rags, just like the next person.
Do you know someone who works hard and never seeks the
praise of others? Let them know you have noticed their hard
work, and give them some praise today.

☐ Pray   ☐ Read   Currently working on _____

Evening Reflection

Day 212

"For where your treasure is, there your heart will be also."

Matthew 6:21

What do you treasure? Take a few minutes to think about the things you treasure before reading on. Do you treasure things or people? Do you treasure yourself or others? Do you treasure the rich or the poor? Do you treasure the strong or the weak? Do you treasure the healthy or the sick? Do you treasure the righteous or the lost? Where was Christ's treasure? Determine today if your treasure is in line with His.

☐ Pray   ☐ Read   Currently working on _____

Evening Reflection

Day 213

"My brethren, count it all joy when you fall into various
trials, knowing that the testing of your faith
produces patience."

James 1:2-3

Tests. Who likes tests? I don't mind them if I do well, but
I can't stand them if I perform poorly. We are faced with
numerous tests each day. Wouldn't you know most of the
tests are exactly the things we struggle with? If you cheat
on schoolwork, you probably have a chance to cheat every
school day. If you struggle with stealing, you probably have an
opportunity to steal each day. If you struggle with pride, you
probably have the chance to brag about yourself daily. How
have your grades been? Have you been failing your tests or
passing them? Today, pick something you struggle with and
use the t-chart on the next page to keep track of how you do
when tested this week. At the end of today, and for the next
six nights, reflect on your day and put marks on the "Pass"
side for when you resisted the temptation and marks on the
"Fail" side for when you gave in. At the end of the week see
how you are doing. Choose to pass today.

Pass	Fail

☐ Pray ☐ Read Currently working on _____

Evening Reflection

Day 214

"And do not fear those who kill the body but cannot kill the soul. But rather fear Him who is able to destroy both soul and body in hell."

Matthew 10:28

This body is only a temporary shell. A relationship with Christ is enough in some places (not often here in the US) to result in physical persecution and even death. Eventually, the persecution we face here will increase. It may be next year or twenty years from now, but either way we must not give in to fear. Today, determine if you think your faith is strong enough to withstand physical persecution.

☐ Pray   ☐ Read   Currently working on _____

Evening Reflection

Day 215

"Do not love the world or the things in the world.
If anyone loves the world, the love of the Father
is not in him."

1 John 2:15

It's quite easy to get caught up in the temptations of this world. Most people would enjoy a lot of money, fame, power, and things of that nature. These things are not a problem unless we love them. We are to love the One who blesses us, not what He blesses us with. Today, determine if you are using the things God has blessed you with for yourself and worldly gains or if you are using them for Him and eternal gains.

☐ Pray   ☐ Read   Currently working on _____

Evening Reflection

235

Day 216

"For if we would judge ourselves,
we would not be judged."

1 Corinthians 11:31

This is not saying if we take it upon ourselves to judge others, then we won't be judged. It is saying if I judge myself, then I won't be judged. Have you ever heard stories of kids who know they did something wrong and who punish themselves in hopes that their parents won't be so hard on them? We have the ability to correct ourselves as believers, but we often don't want to admit we are wrong. Lay your pride down today and reflect on your life to determine what corrections you need to make.

☐ Pray ☐ Read Currently working on _____

Evening Reflection

Day 217

"As we have said before, so now I say again, if anyone preaches any other gospel to you than what you have received, let him be accursed."

Galatians 1:9

Did Jesus preach that there was more than one way to Heaven? Did He not speak the truth because He was afraid He may offend someone? Are your beliefs based on what the Bible says or what someone else tells you? Are you ashamed of your beliefs because they aren't politically correct? Do you try to sugarcoat them? If our beliefs sway with the pendulum of social acceptability, then the Bible is not the core of our beliefs. Today, begin to determine if what you believe is Biblically correct, and be confident in what the word of God says.

☐ Pray   ☐ Read   Currently working on _____

Evening Reflection

Day 218

"If a brother or sister is naked and destitute of daily food, and one of you says to them, 'Depart in peace, be warmed and filled,' but you do not give them the things which are needed for the body, what does it profit?"

James 2:15-16

"I hate to hear it, but I'll be praying for you." "Bless your heart." How many times do we say things like this when we have the power to do more? I've been guilty of doing this. Praying for other people is awesome, but sometimes we toss it around like a "Get Out of Helping Free" card. Find someone in need that you have the ability to help today.

☐ Pray   ☐ Read   Currently working on _____

Evening Reflection

Day 219

"A fool has no delight in understanding,
But in expressing his own heart."

Proverbs 18:2

Have you ever expressed your own heart before you entirely understood a situation? I know I have. Instead of rushing to judgment and offering your opinion about something you hear today, realize you really don't have an understanding of the situation and withhold your input.

☐ Pray   ☐ Read   Currently working on _____

Evening Reflection

Day 220

"Faithful are the wounds of a friend, But the kisses of an enemy are deceitful."

Proverbs 27:6

In other words, it's better to hear the harsh truth from a true friend who cares about you and is looking out for you than to be pampered and babied by a person who truly doesn't care about you. How do you handle constructive criticism from those you know care about you? Do you pridefully push them away, or do you take what they say and evaluate it? Remember today that it is better to be pushed by those who love you than to be comforted by those that don't care.

☐ Pray   ☐ Read   Currently working on _____

Evening Reflection

Day 221

"As each one has received a gift, minister it to one another,
as good stewards of the manifold grace of God."

1 Peter 4:10

God has blessed you with talents. Each one of us have abilities
God has given us. These talents include athletic abilities,
lending a listening ear, being a math wiz, and everything in
between. Are you showing God that you are grateful for His
gracious gifts by using them for His glory? Today, think about
ways you can use your gifts to minister to others.

☐ Pray   ☐ Read   Currently working on _____

Evening Reflection

Day 222

"I set My rainbow in the cloud, and it shall be for the sign
of the covenant between Me and the earth."

Genesis 9:13

Do you know what rainbows symbolize?

Verses 11-12 from the same chapter tell us. They say, "'Thus I
establish My covenant with you: Never again shall all flesh be
cut off by the waters of the flood; never again shall there be a
flood to destroy the earth.' And God said: 'This is the sign of
the covenant which I make between Me and you, and every
living creature that is with you, for perpetual generations:'"

Reading verse 13 again tells us that the rainbow is a sign to
remind us that God promised never to flood the earth again.
Take time to share this with someone today, and next time you
see a rainbow, remember to thank God for this promise.

☐ Pray   ☐ Read   Currently working on _____

Evening Reflection

Day 223

"Better is the poor who walks in his integrity Than one who is perverse in his lips, and is a fool."

Proverbs 19:1

The poorest of the poor have the choice to exhibit integrity or foolishness. If people living in the slums of third world countries can live with integrity, then what is stopping us? It's not about what you attain while you are on this earth, but how you live. Live with integrity today.

☐ Pray   ☐ Read   Currently working on _____

Evening Reflection

Day 224

Tow truck drivers wait for a call to go assist someone. They are on the scene at horrific car wrecks. They bring cars with mechanical problems to the shop. Their job is to respond when others need help. As Christians we have the same job. We are to be there for people during the most difficult times of their lives as well as the smaller issues. When you see a tow truck pray and ask the Lord to help you see those around you who are in need of assistance.

☐ Pray   ☐ Read   Currently working on _____

Evening Reflection

Day 225

"Send Me" by Lecrae should be a wake up call and a
challenge to each of us.

Go to www.StumblingServant.com and click on the Morning
Thoughts Song Challenges link, then Day 225. There you will
find a link to read the lyrics of the song and another to listen
to it. If you don't normally listen to fast paced music, then
I recommend reading the lyrics while the song is playing.
Determine today if you are serving Christ or just practicing
the rituals.

☐ Pray   ☐ Read   Currently working on _____

Evening Reflection

Day 226

"Where there is no wood, the fire goes out; And where there is no talebearer, strife ceases."

Proverbs 26:20

Some of us are good at throwing wood onto the fire or fanning the flames so it grows. Are you one of those people? Avoid fueling conflict today at school, work, or wherever you may go.

☐ Pray ☐ Read Currently working on _____

Evening Reflection

Day 227

"The simple believes every word, But the prudent considers well his steps."

Proverbs 14:15

Do you think about what others are telling you, or do you just accept it as truth? Take time today to think things out and research what others tell you.

☐ Pray   ☐ Read   Currently working on _____

Evening Reflection

Day 228

"pray without ceasing,"

1 Thessalonians 5:17

Don't stop praying. If things are as bad as they have ever been, don't stop praying. If things are as good as they have ever been, don't stop praying. If you have been waiting for a job, don't stop praying. If your health report came back good, don't stop praying. If you are on top of a mountain, don't stop praying. If you are going through a valley, don't stop praying. Each day is full of time we can pray. Look for opportunities to pray today that you normally wouldn't notice.

☐ Pray   ☐ Read   Currently working on _____

Evening Reflection

Day 229

"Therefore, whatever you want men to do to you, do also to them, for this is the Law and the Prophets."

Matthew 7:12

The Golden Rule. Choose someone other than yourself to put in this verse. Therefore, whatever you want men to do to your (mom, dad, husband, wife, son, daughter, friend...), do also to them. Treat everyone you encounter today the way you would want the person you put in the verse to be treated. They may not be *your* mom, dad, husband, wife, son, daughter, or friend, but they are someone's.

☐ Pray   ☐ Read   Currently working on _____

Evening Reflection

Day 230

"But now you yourselves are to put off all these: anger, wrath, malice, blasphemy, filthy language out of your mouth. Do not lie to one another, since you have put off the old man with his deeds, and have put on the new man who is renewed in knowledge according to the image of Him who created him,"

Colossians 3:8-10

If you have a relationship with Christ, are you living like the new you or the old you? A person who has a relationship with Christ will make changes over time. They will not be content with living like they used to. They will want to become more like Christ. Are you content with the person you are? Are there areas in which you wish to improve? If you are perfectly happy with the person you are, then you may want to evaluate the standards you are holding yourself to. Stay away from the deeds of the old man today. Today, strive to become more like Christ-- with the understanding that you will mess up and with confidence He will help you overcome.

☐ Pray   ☐ Read   Currently working on _____

Evening Reflection

Day 231

"Therefore whoever hears these sayings of Mine, and does them, I will liken him to a wise man who built his house on the rock: and the rain descended, the floods came, and the winds blew and beat on that house; and it did not fall, for it was founded on the rock. But everyone who hears these sayings of Mine, and does not do them, will be like a foolish man who built his house on the sand: and the rain descended, the floods came, and the winds blew and beat on that house: and it fell. And great was its fall."

Matthew 7:24-27

Both of these examples hear what they are supposed to do, but only one acts on the instructions. Have you been doing or just hearing? Is your foundation sturdy enough to withstand the storms of life? Today, identify things you need to improve in order to strengthen your foundation of faith.

☐ Pray   ☐ Read   Currently working on _____

Evening Reflection

Day 232

"not with eyeservice, as men-pleasers, but as bondservants of Christ, doing the will of God from the heart,"

Ephesians 6:6

What is the will of God? It is obvious from this verse that it is something we do. Far too often we seek after God's will like it is something we do not know. Don't get me wrong, I'm not saying we know God's plans, and I think we should pray for God's will to take place in our lives. If we aren't careful, however, we end up not doing anything because we aren't sure if it is "God's will" for our life. Simply put, God's will for our life is to love Him and show others His love. Wherever you are today, do just that and leave the rest up to Him.

☐ Pray   ☐ Read   Currently working on ＿＿＿＿＿＿＿

Evening Reflection
＿＿＿＿＿＿＿＿＿＿＿＿＿＿＿＿＿＿＿＿＿
＿＿＿＿＿＿＿＿＿＿＿＿＿＿＿＿＿＿＿＿＿
＿＿＿＿＿＿＿＿＿＿＿＿＿＿＿＿＿＿＿＿＿
＿＿＿＿＿＿＿＿＿＿＿＿＿＿＿＿＿＿＿＿＿
＿＿＿＿＿＿＿＿＿＿＿＿＿＿＿＿＿＿＿＿＿
＿＿＿＿＿＿＿＿＿＿＿＿＿＿＿＿＿＿＿＿＿
＿＿＿＿＿＿＿＿＿＿＿＿＿＿＿＿＿＿＿＿＿
＿＿＿＿＿＿＿＿＿＿＿＿＿＿＿＿＿＿＿＿＿

Day 233

"But God has chosen the foolish things of the world to put to shame the wise, and God has chosen the weak things of the world to put to shame the things which are mighty;"

1 Corinthians 1:27

Are you doing something foolish that would put you to shame if others found out? Have you become so mighty in your own eyes that God is about to use something weak to humble you? Be real with yourself today about how wise and strong you think you are.

☐ Pray   ☐ Read   Currently working on _____

Evening Reflection

Day 234

"Those who sow in tears Shall reap in joy."

Psalm 126:5

It is easier to live for Christ when things are going our way than it is when things aren't. When life's trials come our way, we must continue to do the things God calls us to do despite the tears. Determine today to press on during life's difficult seasons.

☐ Pray   ☐ Read   Currently working on _____

Evening Reflection

Day 235

"So then, my beloved brethren, let every man be swift to hear, slow to speak, slow to wrath; for the wrath of man does not produce the righteousness of God."

James 1:19-20

Our wrath does not produce God's righteousness. Have you ever wanted God to use you to give someone else what you thought they deserve? I know I have. I've been ready and willing a few times. This verse clearly tells us that is not how God works. Rather than being willing to carry out wrath for God, be willing to slow down today.

☐ Pray ☐ Read Currently working on _____

Evening Reflection

Day 236

"Shadrach (Shad-rack), Meshach (Me-shack), and Abed-Nego (A-bend-ego) answered and said to the king, 'O Nebuchadnezzar, we have no need to answer you in this matter. If that is the case, our God whom we serve is able to deliver us from the burning fiery furnace, and He will deliver us from your hand, O king. But if not, let it be known to you, O king, that we do not serve your gods, nor will we worship the gold image which you have set up.'"

Daniel 3:16-18

The king made an image of gold and ordered everyone to bow down and worship it when they heard music being played. Shadrach, Meshach, and Abed-Nego knew that this was not right and refused to bow down and worship the image. The result of not worshiping the image was to be thrown into a fiery furnace. They knew that God could deliver them from the furnace but were not sure if He would or not. They did know, however, that if they were not delivered from the furnace, they would be delivered to Heaven. Shadrach, Meshach, and Abed-Nego weren't the only ones in the crowd who knew it was wrong to bow to the image, but they were the only three not to bow down. Is your faith strong enough right now to stand when others bow? Determine to do what is right in God's eyes and not man's eyes today.

□ Pray   □ Read   Currently working on _____

Evening Reflection

Day 237

"Through wisdom a house is built,
And by understanding it is established;"

Proverbs 24:3

Have you been using wisdom to build your house? If Christ came to inspect your wisdom, would you pass or fail the inspection? Have you been growing in wisdom? Today, ask God to show you the areas of your life you need to reinforce with wisdom.

☐ Pray   ☐ Read   Currently working on _____

Evening Reflection

Day 238

"But I say to you, love your enemies, bless those who curse you, do good to those who hate you, and pray for those who spitefully use you and persecute you,"

Matthew 5:44

Is there someone you think hates you or has used you? Don't take the easy way out and have ill will toward them. Pray for them throughout today, and pray for God to show you how to love them.

☐ Pray   ☐ Read   Currently working on _____

Evening Reflection

Day 239

"Now when they had departed, behold, an angel of the
Lord appeared to Joseph in a dream, saying, 'Arise, take
the young Child and His mother, flee to Egypt, and stay
there until I bring you word; for Herod will seek the young
Child to destroy Him.' When he arose, he took the young
Child and His mother by night and departed for Egypt,"

Matthew 2:13-14

Notice that Joseph took immediate action when he arose
and did not put it off until he got around to it. Obviously he
didn't wait for daylight since the passage says he took them
"by night." How many times do we put off what we know
we should take care of immediately? Don't procrastinate
today.

☐ Pray   ☐ Read   Currently working on _____

Evening Reflection

260

Day 240

Part of Abandon's song "Hero" talks about the choice
Christ made to give His life.

Go to www.StumblingServant.com and click on the Morning
Thoughts Song Challenges link, then Day 240. Links are
provided there for you to read the lyrics to this song and to
listen to it. Remember His choice today.

☐ Pray   ☐ Read   Currently working on _____

Evening Reflection

Day 241

"Pride goes before destruction,
And a haughty spirit before a fall."

Proverbs 16:18

A couple of years ago my mom told me she used to pray that the Lord would protect me from myself while I was growing up. I asked her to keep praying for that. Like most kids I thought I knew it all and that I had everything under control. Looking back, I realize how far from the truth that was. I would much rather address the pride that I have than learn the hard way. Today, ask the Lord to help you see the pride in your life that needs to be addressed.

☐ Pray   ☐ Read   Currently working on _____

Evening Reflection

Day 242

"Do not speak evil of one another, brethren. He who speaks evil of a brother and judges his brother, speaks evil of the law and judges the law. But if you judge the law, you are not a doer of the law but a judge. There is one Lawgiver, who is able to save and to destroy. Who are you to judge another?"

James 4:11-12

I believe this is something we struggle with more than we realize. We usually limit judging someone else to forming an opinion about someone we don't know. There is so much more to it than that. On a daily basis we can judge people's appearance, actions, heart, and intentions. Have you ever said something like, "They are doing it all for show", "He had it all planned out", "She doesn't care", or "He is focused on the wrong thing?" I have said each one of those statements. God is the only one who can accurately judge someone because He is the only one that truly knows people's hearts and intentions. When you say, or think, something judgmental today, quickly correct yourself.

☐ Pray ☐ Read Currently working on _____

Evening Reflection

Day 243

"We have heard with our ears, O God, Our fathers have told us, The deeds You did in their days, In days of old"

Psalm 44:1

Does this take place today? When was the last time you told someone from the younger generation what the Lord has done for you? When was the last time you had an older person tell you about things the Lord has done for them? Telling those close to us what the Lord has done for us is a good thing, but think of how many people are going through something that the Lord has already guided us through. Pray for the Lord to bring someone your way today that needs to hear what He has done for you.

☐ Pray   ☐ Read   Currently working on _____

Evening Reflection

Day 244

"A worthless person, a wicked man, Walks with a perverse mouth; He winks with his eyes, He shuffles his feet, He points with his fingers; Perversity is in his heart, He devises evil continually, He sows discord."

Proverbs 6:12-14

Is God pleased by the things that come out of your mouth? Do you use your words to stir up trouble between people? The things that we say tell a lot about the condition of our heart. If we talk like trash and stir up trouble, then our heart probably needs some work. Ask the Lord to convict you of the things you say today that don't honor Him, and then start making changes.

☐ Pray   ☐ Read   Currently working on _____

Evening Reflection

Day 245

"And these three men, Shadrach, Meshach, and Abed-Nego, fell down bound into the midst of the burning fiery furnace. Then King Nebuchadnezzar was astonished; and he rose in haste and spoke, saying to his counselors, 'Did we not cast three men bound into the midst of the fire?' They answered and said to the king, 'True, O king.' 'Look!' he answered, 'I see four men loose, walking in the midst of the fire; and they are not hurt, and the form of the fourth is like the Son of God.'"

Daniel 3:23-25

Shadrach, Meshach, and Abed-Nego didn't know if the Lord would save them, but they knew He could. They were more concerned that people knew they did not bow down to the idol than they were about their own lives. They showed faith by not bowing down to the idol, but they showed greater faith by not caving in as they got closer to the furnace. It's a lot easier to talk the talk than it is to walk the walk. Do you live the life of a Christian or just talk a good game? Today, walk the walk of someone who has faith that Jesus is present no matter how bad things may seem.

☐ Pray   ☐ Read   Currently working on _____

Evening Reflection

266

Day 246

"Do not grumble against one another, brethren, lest you be condemned. Behold, the Judge is standing at the door!"

James 5:9

We will never be able to accomplish as much as we could for the Lord if we are always involved in drama with each other. If I am sitting arguing with you over whether Jesus had blue eyes or brown eyes, then neither one of us is sharing His love with other people. Today, commit to not engaging in grumbling with fellow believers.

☐ Pray   ☐ Read   Currently working on _____

Evening Reflection

Day 247

"Without counsel, plans go awry, But in the multitude of counselors they are established."

Proverbs 15:22

Do you have a plan to do something? It only takes one hole to sink a big ship. Take time to share your plan with people you trust, and see what kind of input they can offer. If someone begins to tell you, "That will never work" or something else that is an attempt to crush your dreams, then understand that is not the type of counsel you want to pay attention to. Today, make a list of people you can talk to about your plan, and then contact one of them. If you don't have a plan to do anything, then find a need and develop a plan to meet the need.

☐ Pray   ☐ Read   Currently working on _____

Evening Reflection

Day 248

"Now when they saw the boldness of Peter and John, and perceived that they were uneducated and untrained men, they marveled. And they realized that they had been with Jesus."

Acts 4:13

Jesus didn't pick the most educated men to be his disciples. He picked those that didn't make the cut. He picked people that others thought weren't good enough. Peter and John may not have met the standards of the religious people of their time, but they lived boldly for Christ and He used them. Many of us struggle with not being good enough for other people. We think things like, "I'm not pretty enough," "I'm not popular enough," "I'm not rich enough," "I'm not smart enough," and "I'm not funny enough." If you struggle with thoughts like this, fill in the following sentence. I am not _____ enough for _____. Other people's standards can only weigh you down if you choose to carry them. Let go of their standards and allow God to mold you into the person He wants you to be. Live boldly for Christ today, just as you are.

☐ Pray   ☐ Read   Currently working on _____

Evening Reflection

Day 249

"However, Jesus did not permit him, but said to him,
Go home to your friends, and tell them what great
things the Lord has done for you, and how
He has had compassion on you."

Mark 5:19

This verse comes from a passage where a demon-possessed
man was healed. He wanted to leave and go with Jesus, but
Jesus told him to go tell his friends what had been done for
him. When is the last time you told someone what God has
done for you? We need to share with other people how He
has blessed us. This is not to brag out of pride, but to give
Him the credit. Take time today to share something God has
done for you with someone else.

☐ Pray   ☐ Read   Currently working on _____

Evening Reflection

Day 250

"Yes, my inmost being will rejoice
When your lips speak right things."

Proverbs 23:16

Will the things that you say today cause God to rejoice? The words that you speak today have enormous power. They are strong enough to cause your Creator to rejoice. Speak with the right heart today.

☐ Pray   ☐ Read   Currently working on _____

Evening Reflection

Day 251

Monthly Prayer

Saturday nights here in America are Sunday mornings in other parts of the world. As we prepare to go to bed, there are pastors getting ready to share the Word of God with others. There are missionaries preparing to baptize people in a river or tub. There are Christians inviting family, friends, and coworkers to attend church with them. There are people traveling to underground churches where they could be killed if people found out what they were doing. There are also broken people who are ready to give up and do not know where to turn. Pray for all of these people. Pray that the Lord would speak through those that will be speaking. Pray that Christians would have a burden to share Christ with those they have contact with. Pray that those who are broken will find their way to a place where they will hear about the love of Christ.

☐ Pray   ☐ Read   Currently working on _____

Evening Reflection

Day 252

"For do I now persuade men, or God? Or do I seek to please men? For if I still pleased men, I would not be a bondservant of Christ."

Galatians 1:10

Are you seeking to please people or to please God? Take a minute to think about this. Do you go to church to please your spouse/parents/kids or because you desire to learn more about Christ? Do you work hard in order to get that promotion or because God wants you to? Do you help others to impress someone or because God commanded you to? Let everything you do today please the Lord.

☐ Pray   ☐ Read   Currently working on _____

Evening Reflection

Day 253

"Finally, my brethren, be strong in the Lord and in the power of His might. Put on the whole armor of God, that you may be able to stand against the wiles of the devil. For we do not wrestle against flesh and blood, but against principalities, against powers, against the rulers of the darkness of this age, against spiritual hosts of wickedness in the heavenly places. Therefore take up the whole armor of God, that you may be able to withstand in the evil day, and having done all, to stand...above all, taking the shield of faith with which you will be able to quench all the fiery darts of the wicked one."

Ephesians 6:10-13,16

This verse tells us that we will be attacked. It's not a matter of if, but when. How smart would it be to go into battle without a shield? We must have faith in the Lord and trust that He knows what He is doing. We will not always understand things, but we must stay faithful to Him. No matter what you are going through, or how good things may be going, pick up the shield of faith today and stand prepared to face whatever is thrown your way.

☐ Pray   ☐ Read   Currently working on _____

Evening Reflection

Day 254

"Now Jesus sat opposite the treasury and saw how the people put money into the treasury. And many who were rich put in much. The one poor widow came and threw in two mites, which make a quadrans, So he called his disciples to Himself and said to them, 'Assuredly, I say to you that this poor widow has put in more than all those who have given to the treasury; for they all put in out of their abundance, but she out of her poverty put in all that she had, her whole livelihood.'"

Mark 12:41-44

How much are you really giving back to God? Today, compare how much you give back to God in one month and how much you spend on extra stuff. If you think you give enough, then continue. If you think you can do more, then find a missionary or ministry to support.

☐ Pray ☐ Read Currently working on _____

Evening Reflection

Day 255

Kari Jobe's song "We Are" talks about what we are called to do as Christians.

Go to www.StumblingServant.com and click on the Morning Thoughts Song Challenges link, then Day 255. There you will be able to watch a performance of this song. After watching the video, evaluate how bright your light is shining.

☐ Pray   ☐ Read   Currently working on _____

Evening Reflection

Day 256

"There is one who scatters, yet increases more;
And there is one who withholds more than is right,
But it leads to poverty."

Proverbs 11:24

Do you hoard all the things God has blessed you with, or do you use them to help others? This verse talks about two paths. Which one will you take today?

☐ Pray   ☐ Read   Currently working on _____

Evening Reflection

Day 257

"If the foot should say, 'Because I am not a hand, I am not of the body,' is it therefore not of the body? And if the ear should say, 'Because I am not an eye, I am not of the body,' is it therefore not of the body? If the whole body were an eye, where would be the hearing? If the whole were hearing, where would be the smelling? But now God has set the members, each one of them, in the body just as He pleased. And if they were all one member, where would the body be?"

1 Corinthians 12:15-19

You have an important job in the body of Christ, and the Lord handpicked you for it. No part is insignificant. When one of us slacks off, it affects the whole body. The body can not be as strong as it should be and work as it is intended to work unless we all do our part. What talents has the Lord given you? We don't all have amazing voices, great athletic ability, or keen business knowledge, but the Lord has given us all some sort of talent. Today, while you are at school, work, shopping, at the gym, or wherever you may be, remember that your actions and attitude affect the body of Christ.

☐ Pray   ☐ Read   Currently working on _____

Evening Reflection

Day 258

"bearing with one another, and forgiving one another, if anyone has a complaint against another; even as Christ forgave you, so you also must do."

Colossians 3:13

This is one of those verses many of us us don't like to acknowledge. "Must" is a very definitive word, and we don't like being told we have to do something. Christ tells us here we have to forgive others. Let's be clear, He does not say we have to trust those who have done us wrong, but we must forgive them. If you have been in an abusive relationship, or are in one, do not go back or continue in it because you feel that is required in order to forgive the person. That is not the case. Today, determine what you are holding in your heart that you need to forgive others for.

☐ Pray ☐ Read   Currently working on _____

Evening Reflection

Day 259

"Blessed be the God and Father of our Lord Jesus Christ,
the Father of mercies and God of all comfort, who
comforts us in all our tribulation, that we may be able to
comfort those who are in any trouble, with the comfort
with which we ourselves are comforted by God."

2 Corinthians 1:3-4

This verse tells us that we need to comfort others during their
times of trial in the same way the Lord comforts us. Have you
been the victim of physical abuse? Have you lost a child? Has
your spouse left you or passed away? Have you dealt with a
deadly disease? Have you struggled with substance abuse?
The Lord can turn our trials into ministries, if we allow Him
to. We can't all relate to what others are going through, but
we can relate to others who are going through valleys we
have walked through. Are you willing to allow the Lord to
turn your trials into a ministry? Today, think back to what
comforted you during your trials, and start looking for others
going through similar situations.

☐ Pray   ☐ Read   Currently working on _____

Evening Reflection

Day 260

"Death and life are in the power of the tongue, And those who love it will eat its fruit."

Proverbs 18:21

Death and life are serious stuff. We may not physically kill someone with our tongue, but what about the dreams of other people? Have you ever killed someone's dreams by saying, "You should just give up on it?" Our words can also offer hope to those who need encouragement. Use your tongue to speak life today.

☐ Pray   ☐ Read   Currently working on _____

Evening Reflection

Day 261

"If you love Me, keep My commandments."

John 14:15

Do you love Christ? How well do you keep His commandments? Do you know what His commandments are? If not, take time today to research His commandments. If you know what they are, identify the ones you need to work on.

☐ Pray ☐ Read Currently working on _____

Evening Reflection

Day 262

"Therefore do not worry about tomorrow, for tomorrow will worry about its own things. Sufficient for the day is its own trouble."

Matthew 6:34

Sometimes I struggle with looking to tomorrow instead of focusing on today. Whether it is doing something with friends, planning an event, or just wondering how things will work out, we have to remember that each day has its own challenges. If our focus is on something down the road, we are more likely to slip up. Stay focused on doing your part today, and pray that the Lord will prepare you today for what will come tomorrow.

☐ Pray   ☐ Read   Currently working on _____

Evening Reflection

Day 263

"Then the Lord said to him, 'Now you Pharisees make the outside of the cup and dish clean, but your inward part is full of greed and wickedness.'"

Luke 11:39

We must be careful of labeling a person a Pharisee. More importantly, we must make sure we are not one ourselves. Remember, God looks at the inward appearance. Make sure that what He is seeing today pleases Him, rather than trying to impress others with your outside appearance and possessions.

☐ Pray   ☐ Read   Currently working on ＿＿＿＿＿＿＿

Evening Reflection

Day 264

"Wash me thoroughly from my iniquity,
And cleanse me from my sin."

Psalm 51:2

This should be a daily prayer for all of us. Are you ready to be washed of the things you do that you know you shouldn't be doing, or are you content going back to them time and again? Are you ready to be cleansed of the unwillingness that holds you back from doing the things you know you should be doing? Are you prepared for the Lord to reveal your actions and aspects of life that are displeasing to Him? Today, ask the Lord to convict your heart of the things you do that you shouldn't, the things you don't do that you should, and the things you do or don't do that you aren't aware of yet.

☐ Pray   ☐ Read   Currently working on _____

Evening Reflection

Day 265

"Yea, though I walk through the valley of the shadow of death, I will fear no evil; For You are with me; Your rod and Your staff, they comfort me."

Psalm 23:4

Can you claim this? I know there have been times in my life where I may have acted like this, but it was out of pride and ignorance rather than faith. We shouldn't fear--not because of who we are, but because of who God is. Today, evaluate if your confidence is in yourself or in the Lord.

☐ Pray   ☐ Read   Currently working on _____

Evening Reflection

Day 266

"I have made a covenant with my eyes; Why then should I look upon a young woman?"

Job 31:1

One peek can turn into total embrace. Identify the things that tempt you when you look at them today, and make a covenant with your eyes not to look at them.

☐ Pray ☐ Read Currently working on _____

Evening Reflection

Day 267

"A man's heart plans his way, But the LORD
directs his steps."

Proverbs 16:9

Have you ever been carried away with your plans? Is there
something you are planning right now? If you have plans,
spend today praying that God would demolish your plan if it
is not what He wants you to do. If you don't have plans, pray
for plans that are in line with God's direction.

☐ Pray   ☐ Read   Currently working on _____

Evening Reflection

Day 268

"To do righteousness and justice
Is more acceptable to the Lord than sacrifice."

Proverbs 21:3

Today, be righteous and just.

☐ Pray   ☐ Read   Currently working on _____

Evening Reflection

Day 269

"Everyone proud in heart is an abomination to the LORD;
Though they join forces, none will go unpunished."

Proverbs 16:5

If this verse isn't reason enough to get rid of our pride, I don't
know what is. Evaluate how prideful you are today.

☐ Pray ☐ Read Currently working on _____

Evening Reflection

Day 270

Casting Crowns' song "Until The Whole World Hears"
talks about wanting to serve Christ and set
an example for Him.

Go to www.StumblingServant.com and click on the Morning
Thoughts Song Challenges link, then Day 270. There you will
find links to read the lyrics to this song, to listen to it, and
to watch the music video for it. Today, let the prayer in this
song be your prayer.

☐ Pray   ☐ Read   Currently working on _____

Evening Reflection

Day 271

"Professing to be wise, they became fools,"

Romans 1:22

Are you into self-promoting? How often do you talk about yourself and the things you are good at? Don't allow yourself to fall into the trap of thinking that you are anything other than a tool used by God. If given the opportunity to brag about yourself today, let it pass by.

☐ Pray   ☐ Read   Currently working on ＿＿＿＿＿＿

Evening Reflection

Day 272

"The eyes of the Lord are in every place,
Keeping watch on the evil and the good."

Proverbs 15:3

The Lord will see you at school today. The Lord will see you at work today. The Lord will see you watching TV today. The Lord will see you driving down the road today. The Lord will see you at the store today. The Lord will see you on the computer today. The Lord will see you be kind today. The Lord will see you make fun of others today. The Lord will see you pray today. The Lord will see you disrespect others today. The Lord will see you help someone today. The Lord will see you use drugs today. The Lord will see you study His Word today. No matter where you go today, the Lord will see you. No matter what you do today, the Lord will see it. Before you go somewhere or do something today, ask yourself if you want the Lord to see it.

☐ Pray   ☐ Read   Currently working on _____

Evening Reflection

Day 273

"I beseech you therefore, brethren, by the mercies of God, that you present your bodies a living sacrifice, holy, acceptable to God, which is your reasonable service."

Romans 12:1

Reasonable service is not the way we like to look at things. We like to feel good about ourselves when we spend time reading His Word or praying. We like to think we are doing Him a favor when we choose to do things His way. We drop some money in the offering plate and think we are stretching ourselves. Although all of these are great practices, it is our reasonable service to do them. We shouldn't feel like we need an award or attention for doing things we are supposed to do. Do the things you know He would have you to do today, without feeling like you are doing something special.

☐ Pray   ☐ Read   Currently working on _____

Evening Reflection

Day 274

"Brethren, if anyone among you wanders from the truth, and someone turns him back, let him know that he who turns a sinner from the error of his way will save a soul from death and cover a multitude of sins."

James 5:19-20

Remember, I am not a Biblical scholar. I am not sure if this verse is talking about believers or non-believers. In my humble opinion, it truly does not matter because we all know both types of people. Today, pray for God to open a door and allow you to share His truth with someone who has not accepted it, as well as to encourage a believer who has wandered away. He can open the doors, but it is up to us to walk through them.

☐ Pray   ☐ Read   Currently working on _____

Evening Reflection

Day 275

"The discretion of a man makes him slow to anger,
And his glory is to overlook a transgression."

Proverbs 19:11

How often do you overlook situations you could cause a fuss over? Are you waiting for someone to do you wrong one more time so you can tell them off? Do you go off on people for honest mistakes? Choose to overlook things you could get upset about today.

☐ Pray   ☐ Read   Currently working on _____

Evening Reflection

Day 276

"But Peter said, 'Man, I do not know what you are saying!'
Immediately, while he was still speaking, the rooster crowed.
And the Lord turned and looked at Peter. Then Peter
remembered the word of the Lord, how He had said to him,
'Before the rooster crows, you will deny Me three times.'"

Luke 22:60-61

Have you ever felt like you let the Lord down? Peter had
to feel like he was scraping rock bottom when that rooster
crowed. Let's read a verse from three days later. Luke 24:12
says, "But Peter arose and ran to the tomb; and stooping
down, he saw the linen cloths lying by themselves; and he
departed, marveling to himself at what had happened." I'm
sure Peter was upset with himself, but he did not allow it to
keep him down. Within three days he was running to the
empty tomb. Have you failed the Lord? I know I have. Are
you still down about it? Maybe it was yesterday, last week, or
three years ago. We will be down as long as we choose to be
down. What if Peter had hidden for a week because he was
ashamed? He wouldn't have been able to run to the tomb
and find it empty. If we aren't careful, we will miss being a
part of great things by not getting back up and moving on.
Today is a new day. Choose to get over past failures today
and to run toward Him.

☐ Pray   ☐ Read   Currently working on _____

Evening Reflection

Day 277

"It is honorable for a man to stop striving,
Since any fool can start a quarrel."

Proverbs 20:3

It doesn't take much to start or participate in an argument,
but it takes self-control to walk away from one. Refuse to be
involved in any quarrels today.

☐ Pray   ☐ Read   Currently working on _____

Evening Reflection

Day 278

"It is good neither to eat meat nor drink wine nor do anything by which your brother stumbles or is offended or is made weak."

Romans 14:21

How often do we think about the way our everyday actions affect others? If our co-workers are trying to eat healthier and we always get them to go eat fast food with us for lunch, then we are a stumbling block for them. Today, find out something someone around you is trying to improve, and see how you can help.

☐ Pray   ☐ Read   Currently working on _____

Evening Reflection

Day 279

Monthly Prayer

With all of the technology and social media we have these days, it does not take long for the news of tragedy to spread. I think we can become numb to the horrible things we hear due to the simple fact that we hear them so often. We now have the ability to share news as it is literally taking place. It is hard to believe how fast footage and pictures of natural disasters can travel from one side of the world to the other. I wonder if we have become so caught up in breaking news through our social media accounts that we forget to take time and pray for those involved. Are we more worried about being the first one to post something than we are about the people affected by these tragedies? It doesn't matter if it is an earthquake, baby drowning, terrorist attack, or fatal car accident, these events change real people's lives. We literally watch things on TV that other people are living through. From now on, when you hear bad news, stop and pray for those involved before you rush to share it with someone else.

☐ Pray   ☐ Read   Currently working on _____

Evening Reflection

Day 280

"Therefore submit to God. Resist the devil and
he will flee from you."

James 4:7

How many of us who profess to be Christians are submitting
to the devil and resisting God these days? My first thought
was that you can't resist the devil and not be submitting to
God. That is true, but it goes further than that. Are you only
submitting to God when you resist the evil things the devil
throws at you? If so, that is not enough. We must submit to
God in all things; not just when we need to find a way out
of temptation. Today, dive in and totally submit yourself to
God.

☐ Pray   ☐ Read   Currently working on _____

Evening Reflection

Day 281

"So it was, when the Philistine arose and came and drew near to meet David, that David hurried and ran toward the army to meet the Philistine."

1 Samuel 17:48

David did not waver. He did not hesitate. He did not second-guess the situation. He had a giant in his life, and he ran toward it. He did not run to Goliath with pride, but with faith. That faith was not in his abilities or past victories, but in his God. We all face giants at one point or another. Are you facing a giant now? If so, how are you dealing with it? Is your faith in the Lord, or are you trying everything you can possibly think of to take care of it yourself? If not, do you know of anyone else who is facing a giant? Are you doing what you can to help them, or are you discouraging them like people tried to discourage David? Today, evaluate how you are facing the giant in your life, or how you are helping someone else who is facing a giant.

☐ Pray   ☐ Read   Currently working on _____

Evening Reflection

Day 282

"Train up a child in the way he should go,
And when he is old he will not depart from it."

Proverbs 22:6

"Train up a child" does not mean take them to church a few times a week. It doesn't mean send them to church camp for a week of the summer. People don't train for the Olympics a few hours a week. They don't set one week of the year aside to get better. They train daily. Kids these days are trained in the ways of the world almost non-stop. How much training are they getting from you? Are you teaching them how to pray? Do you let them see you reading your Bible? Do you have conversations about faith? I have two young nephews, and my brother-in-law and sister are teaching their oldest about Christ. Are you leaving the training of your children up to other people? Today, evaluate how much training you have been doing. If you have young kids, be active in training them. If you have older kids and didn't do as much training as you wish you had, then have a conversation with them about it today. Determine today to help train the children around you.

☐ Pray   ☐ Read   Currently working on _____

Evening Reflection

Day 283

"To show partiality is not good, Because for a piece of bread a man will transgress."

Proverbs 28:21

Have you placed anyone up on a pedestal? Is there someone that you think really has it together? None of us are above messing up. This verse is saying that it doesn't take much for someone to falter. We set ourselves up for hurt when we place people on pedestals. Your mom, dad, brother, sister, teacher, coach, friends, pastor, youth pastor, son, daughter, and others that are special to you are all human. We are all capable of ending up on the front page of the paper for making a bad decision. Although the odds of that happening may not be high, we can be sure that those we look up to will upset us at some point. Take time today to see if you are holding anyone to non-human expectations, and make up your mind to forgive those who have made and will make mistakes.

☐ Pray ☐ Read Currently working on _____

Evening Reflection

Day 284

"For I say, through the grace given to me, to everyone who is among you, not to think of himself more highly than he ought to think, but to think soberly, as God has dealt to each one a measure of faith."

Romans 12:3

"To each one" means to everyone, right? So if everyone received something, how does anyone have more than another? This passage goes on to talk about how we are the body of Christ. It says we don't all have the same talents and gifts, but we are all needed. The water boy is just as important as the coach. He may not get paid as much, but if the team doesn't stay hydrated, how well are they going to play? You may say, "Well, the coach can make the water." You're right, but who is going to coach the team while he is making the water? Who is going to prepare a game plan while he washes out the coolers? We all have jobs, and all of them are important. Today, realize that you are special to God, but not more special than anyone else.

☐ Pray   ☐ Read   Currently working on _____

Evening Reflection

Day 285

Jason Gray's song "More Like Falling in Love" addresses some distinctions we should all be aware of.

Go to www.StumblingServant.com and click on the Morning Thoughts Song Challenges link, then Day 285. There you will find a link to listen to this song. Today, compare the reasons behind your faith to the ones in this song.

☐ Pray   ☐ Read   Currently working on _____

Evening Reflection

Day 286

"For the love of money is a root of all kinds of evil, for
which some have strayed from the faith in their greediness,
and pierced themselves through with many sorrows."

1 Timothy 6:10

Do you love money? Has money changed the person you
are? Has it caused you to stray from your faith? Sometimes
we become focused on something and do not realize how
far we have drifted from who we once were. Along the way
it is possible to sell ourselves out. Take time today to see if
you have strayed from your faith and the person you once
were for the love of money.

☐ Pray   ☐ Read   Currently working on _____

Evening Reflection

Day 287

"And my God shall supply all your need according to
His riches in glory by Christ Jesus."

Philippians 4:19

The majority of Americans need five things on a daily basis. We need food, drink, housing, clothes, and transportation. Needing food does not mean I need lobster or steak. Needing something to drink does not mean I need a Dr. Pepper or a Pepsi. Needing housing does not mean I need a 3,500 square foot home. Needing clothing does not mean I need Gucci or Polo clothes. Needing transportation does not mean I need a new Viper or Bentley. Think about how much money we could use to help others if we didn't think we needed everything to be top of the line. If you have more food than rice and corn to eat, purified water to drink, sleep in a structurally sound place, have clothes without holes in them (including the ones you paid for with holes in them), and a car to drive, then your needs are beyond met. Today, go to Bing, or another search engine, and search "how many people die because of a lack of food or clean water." Search "slum houses." Search what percentage of the world owns a car. After searching these things, determine if you are willing to cut back in any areas in order to help meet the real needs of others.

☐ Pray ☐ Read Currently working on _____

Evening Reflection

Day 288

Forsake foolishness and live, And go in the way of understanding."

Proverbs 9:6

There is a difference between asking forgiveness for being foolish and forsaking foolishness. There is a difference between telling your spouse, employer, child, parents, friends, or God that you are sorry and actually not doing it again. We have to understand that asking for forgiveness is good, but continuing with the same actions will lead to consequences that we would have avoided had we chosen to quit being foolish. Today, determine if there is anything you need to quit asking forgiveness for, and truly forsake.

☐ Pray ☐ Read Currently working on _____

Evening Reflection

Day 289

"As the Father loved Me, I also have loved you;
abide in My love."

John 15:9

Have you been living in the love of Jesus, or have you been living in the ways of this world? Before you act today, think about if your actions will reflect the love of Christ.

☐ Pray ☐ Read Currently working on _____

Evening Reflection

Day 290

"A prudent man foresees evil and hides himself;
The simple pass on and are punished."

Proverbs 27:12

What do you do when you see that something bad could come out of a situation? Do you excuse yourself from the situation, or do you go with the flow? Today, when the opportunity to do something you shouldn't do presents itself, choose not to do it.

☐ Pray ☐ Read Currently working on _____

Evening Reflection

Day 291

"But the wisdom that is from above is first pure, then peaceable, gentle, willing to yield, full of mercy and good fruits, without partiality, and without hypocrisy."

James 3:17

If we want to be wise, we have to live out the attributes listed in this verse. My wife probably does a better job living these attributes out than I do. Write these traits down and look at them a couple times today while praying for God to help you live them out.

☐ Pray   ☐ Read   Currently working on _____

Evening Reflection

Day 292

"Make yourself an ark of gopherwood; make rooms in the ark, and cover it inside and outside with pitch."

Genesis 6:14

As hard as it is, try to imagine that it had never rained. Now try to imagine that God told you to build an ark because it was going to rain. How would you react? Would you react like I probably would and ask what an ark and rain were in order to see if you could come up with a better idea? Would you be willing to build it? Would you be willing to continue to build it after people start to ridicule you for doing it? God may be asking you to do something today that is going to help down the road. Do you trust Him enough to do it? Today, evaluate your level of trust in Christ.

☐ Pray   ☐ Read   Currently working on _____

Evening Reflection

Day 293

"Now they came to Jericho. As He went out of Jericho with His disciples and a great multitude, blind Bartimaeus, the son of Timaeus, sat by the road begging. And when he heard that it was Jesus of Nazareth, he began to cry out and say, 'Jesus, Son of David, have mercy on me!' Then many warned him to be quiet; but he cried out all the more, 'Son of David, have mercy on me!' So Jesus stood still and commanded him to be called. Then they called the blind man, saying to him, 'Be of good cheer. Rise, He is calling you.' And throwing aside his garment, he rose and came to Jesus. So Jesus answered and said to him, 'What do you want Me to do for you?' The blind man said to Him, 'Rabboni, that I may receive my sight.' Then Jesus said to him, 'Go your way; your faith has made you well.' And immediately he received his sight and followed Jesus on the road."

Mark 10:46-52

How desperate are you for Jesus to help you with your struggles? We do not all have health struggles, but we all have life struggles. Bartimaeus was willing to cry out for help. He wasn't concerned by what others thought about him. He knew this was his chance to be healed, and he wasn't going to let others tell him to be quiet. If Jesus was to walk down the center of your city, would you have the courage to go seek His help? Would you continue to cry out despite the threats of others? I kind of doubt many of us would. I say that due to the fact that often we won't go pray at the alter at church because we are worried what others will think. Sure we will all raise our hands saying we have an unspoken prayer request, but hardly any of us go speak that request to God when given the opportunity to do so. Don't allow what others may think to stop you from doing something the Lord wants you to do today.

☐ Pray   ☐ Read   Currently working on _____

Evening Reflection

Day 294

"Do all things without complaining, and disputing,"

Philippians 2:14

How often do you complain? We do it more than we realize. We complain when someone puts pickles on a burger when we told them we didn't want any, when our computer isn't working fast enough, or when the church service lasts 5 minutes longer than normal. When you start to complain about something today, don't do it.

☐ Pray ☐ Read Currently working on _____

Evening Reflection

Day 295

"For His anger is but for a moment, His favor is for life;
Weeping may endure for a night, But joy comes
in the morning."

Psalm 30:5

Joy is here this very morning. No matter what you are going through today, be joyful in knowing that God's favor is forever.

☐ Pray ☐ Read Currently working on _____

Evening Reflection

Day 296

"He who tills his land will have plenty of bread, But he who follows frivolity will have poverty enough!"

Proverbs 28:19

Have you been tilling your land, or have you been going about life with a careless attitude? If we want to grow in any area of our lives, we must be willing to put in the work that is necessary. A farmer can't just drop some seeds on the dirt and expect everything else to take care of itself. Is Christ pleased with the amount of work you are putting into your life? Determine today if you are tilling your land or just dropping seeds.

☐ Pray   ☐ Read   Currently working on _____

Evening Reflection

Day 297

"Let brotherly love continue. Do not forget to entertain strangers, for by so doing some have unwittingly entertained angels. Remember the prisoners as if chained with them—those who are mistreated—since you yourselves are in the body also."

Hebrews 13:1-3

"Remember the prisoners." What are your thoughts of prisoners? Does your perception of someone change when you hear they were in prison? No matter how "little" you have done and how "much" a prisoner has done, we are all sinners in the eyes of Christ. Today, be in prayer for someone that you know is in prison. If you don't know of anyone, then go to Google, or another search engine, and search the news for "sent to prison." Pray for a name that comes up.

☐ Pray   ☐ Read   Currently working on _____

Evening Reflection

Day 298

"Listen to counsel and receive instruction,
That you may be wise in your latter days."

Proverbs 19:20

"In your latter days." Odds are that you don't know everything yet, and if you think you do, then you still have more to learn. The more of this book I work on, the more I realize how far I have to go. You don't accept Christ as your savior and immediately gain all the wisdom you will ever have. It is a process, a life-long process. Don't worry about how far you have to go. Just be better today than you were yesterday.

☐ Pray   ☐ Read   Currently working on _____

Evening Reflection

Day 299

"As Peter was coming in, Cornelius met him and fell down at his feet and worshiped him. But Peter lifted him up, saying, 'Stand up; I myself am also a man.'"

Acts 10:25-26

If you're the popular kid at school, the star of your team, the CEO of a company, the head of the PTA, the manager at your job, a legendary coach, an award-winning entertainer, the smartest kid in your class, or anything else that someone else may want to be, how do you deal with it? Do you allow others to feed your ego and treat you as if you are better than everyone else? If this is you, insist on being treated normally today. If it isn't you, be thankful you don't have others feeding your pride.

☐ Pray ☐ Read Currently working on _____

Evening Reflection

Day 300

Kerrie Roberts' song "No Matter What" talks about
having faith that is unshakeable.

Go to www.StumblingServant.com and click on the Morning
Thoughts Song Challenges link, then Day 300. There you will
find a link to read the lyrics to this song and another link to
listen to it. Determine today if your faith is strong enough
to live by these words.

☐ Pray   ☐ Read   Currently working on _____

Evening Reflection

Day 301

"And so it was, when Moses held up his hand, that Israel prevailed; and when he let down his hand, Amalek prevailed. But Moses' hands became heavy; so they took a stone and put it under him, and he sat on it. And Aaron and Hur supported his hands, one on one side, and the other on the other side; and his hands were steady until the going down of the sun."

Exodus 17:11-12

No matter how strong we are, sometimes we get tired. It is important to have friends we can depend on during those times. Moses did all he could, but without Aaron and Hur, the Israelites would have lost the battle. Do you have friends you can depend on when your burden becomes heavy? Are you a help to others when they can no longer continue on their own? God has placed us in people's lives and put people in our lives to do exactly this. Find someone you can support today.

☐ Pray ☐ Read Currently working on _____

Evening Reflection

Day 302

"But the fruit of the Spirit is love, joy, peace, longsuffering
(patience), kindness, goodness, faithfulness, gentleness,
self-control. Against such there is no law."

Galatians 5:22-23

Our lives should have evidence of these nine character traits.
If the people closest to you were given a survey asking to rate
you from 1-10 in each of these areas, what would your ratings
look like? Which of these nine areas do you struggle with?
Identify the areas that you need to improve in today. Ask the
Lord to help you see ways you can improve, and search His
Word for guidance.

☐ Pray   ☐ Read   Currently working on _____

Evening Reflection

Day 303

"At that time Jesus went through the grainfields on the Sabbath. And His disciples were hungry, and began to pluck heads of grain and to eat. And when the Pharisees saw it, they said to Him, 'Look, Your disciples are doing what is not lawful to do on the Sabbath!'"

Matthew 12:1-2

The Pharisees were watching for the disciples to "mess up." Although they did nothing wrong this time in Jesus' eyes, the Pharisees still took advantage of the opportunity.Don't forget that people are watching you. They may or may not be waiting for you to "mess up," but they are still paying attention. Make sure they see actions that reflect well on Christ today.

☐ Pray   ☐ Read   Currently working on _____

Evening Reflection

Day 304

"Say to them: 'As I live,' says the Lord GOD, 'I have no pleasure in the death of the wicked, but that the wicked turn from his way and live. Turn, turn from your evil ways! For why should you die, O house of Israel?'"

Ezekiel 33:11

Have you ever prayed that the Lord would take the life of someone who was truly wicked? With all of the evil going on these days, I know I have. I have prayed that God would take the life of anyone who is planning to bring intentional harm to another person. After thinking about this a while back, I no longer pray the same prayer. Now I pray that the wicked would turn from their evil ways, and if they do not, that the Lord would take their life before they harm others. Take time today to sincerely pray for the wicked to turn from their evil ways.

☐ Pray   ☐ Read   Currently working on _____

Evening Reflection

Day 305

"And you will be hated by all for My name's sake."

Luke 21:17

Are you willing to be hated by all? What person throughout history do you think is hated most? Are you willing to live for Christ if it means being hated by more people than the person you thought of? This is a very deep question. Read Luke 21:7-19 and reflect on this today.

☐ Pray   ☐ Read   Currently working on _____

Evening Reflection

Day 306

"But if we hope for what we do not see, we eagerly wait for it with perseverance."

Romans 8:25

Is there something that you are eagerly waiting for? Don't give up hope. Keep your eyes on God, and know that His timing is perfect. Today, be patient knowing that God will meet our needs in His time.

☐ Pray ☐ Read Currently working on _____

Evening Reflection

Day 307

No one loves to be cruising along at about 70 mph before coming to a dead stop because of road construction. No one likes it at the time, but if the work is done right, we normally realize things are better than they were before the construction started. Instead of bobbing and weaving between lanes to try to get a few cars ahead, use the time to ask the Lord to work on you. Ask Him to help you see the potholes in your life that need to be filled in. Ask Him to show you the bumps that need to be smoothed out. Pray for Him to continue to work on you so that you can become more like Him.

☐ Pray   ☐ Read   Currently working on _____

Evening Reflection

Day 308

"But beware lest somehow this liberty of yours become a stumbling block to those who are weak. For if anyone sees you who have knowledge eating in an idol's temple, will not the conscience of him who is weak be emboldened to eat those things offered to idols?"

1 Corinthians 8:9-10

As a Christian, people should be able to watch us and have an example of how to live a life that is pleasing to God. Odds are that today you probably won't eat food offered to an idol, but what else may you do that could set a bad example? Today, live with the knowledge that those around you may live their life based on how you live yours.

☐ Pray   ☐ Read   Currently working on _____

Evening Reflection

Day 309

"When I have brought them to the land flowing with milk and honey, of which I swore to their fathers, and they have eaten and filled themselves and grown fat, then they will turn to other gods and serve them; and they will provoke Me and break My covenant."

Deuteronomy 31:20

Does this sound familiar? Look around our country, maybe even in the mirror. Compared to the rest of the world, those of us in America are very fat--and I'm not talking about physically. When the bank account is full, when there is food in the refrigerator, when the car is running well, and when everyone is healthy, it is easy to become comfortable and slack off living for Christ. It seems we run back to Christ once one of those things is in danger. Have you become fat and unthankful for all Christ has given you? Do you think you have it rough because the air conditioner in your car is broken or because your internet connection is down? Seek after Christ today as if you were desperate for Him.

☐ Pray   ☐ Read   Currently working on _____

Evening Reflection

Day 310

"Greater love has no one than this, than to lay down
one's life for his friends."

John 15:13

Would you be willing to give up your life for a friend? I hope
that I would, but I can't say I know that I would. Let's look
at "lay down one's life" from a different perspective. How
willing would you be to set aside whatever you were doing if a
friend called and was in a bind? Would it depend on who the
friend was? If we aren't willing to set aside something we are
doing to go help a friend, then what are the odds we would
physically give up our life for theirs? Set aside something you
want to do, in order to help a friend out today.

☐ Pray   ☐ Read   Currently working on _____

Evening Reflection

Day 311

"As charcoal is to burning coals, and wood to fire, So is a contentious man to kindle strife,"

Proverbs 26:21

How contentious are you? Some of us are known for being at the center of controversy or being involved in arguments. Whether you are working out at the gym, eating on your lunch break, or whatever else you may do, choose not to be an advocate for confrontation today.

☐ Pray   ☐ Read   Currently working on _____

Evening Reflection

Day 312

"And when Pharaoh drew near, the children of Israel lifted their eyes, and behold, the Egyptians marched after them. So they were very afraid, and the children of Israel cried out to the LORD." "And Moses said to the people, 'Do not be afraid. Stand still, and see the salvation of the LORD, which He will accomplish for you today. For the Egyptians whom you see today, you shall see again no more forever. The LORD will fight for you, and you shall hold your peace.'" "So the children of Israel went into the midst of the sea on the dry ground, and the waters were a wall to them on their right hand and on their left."

Exodus 14:10,13-14, and 22

Do you feel cornered? The children of Israel certainly did. The Lord provided them with a cloud during the day and a pillar of fire during the night to lead them to freedom. Soon after, Pharaoh began to chase them. From one direction the children of Israel were being chased by the Egyptians, and in the other direction was the Red Sea. They had nowhere to go and were questioning why they even left Egypt. The Lord gave them their freedom, but they were wishing they were still slaves. Have you ever asked God to do something, and when He began to do it, you weren't so sure you wanted it anymore? No matter how bleak a situation may look, He will provide a way for you. It is up to us to trust and follow Him. Be courageous, stand still, and ask God to work for you today.

☐ Pray   ☐ Read   Currently working on _____

Evening Reflection

Day 313

"Then Jesus answered and said: A certain man went down from Jerusalem to Jericho, and fell among thieves, who stripped him of his clothing, wounded him, and departed, leaving him half dead. Now by chance a certain priest came down that road. And when he saw him, he passed by on the other side. Likewise a Levite, when he arrived at the place, came and looked, and passed by on the other side. But a certain Samaritan, as he journeyed, came where he was. And when he saw him, he had compassion. So he went to him and bandaged his wounds, pouring on oil and wine; and he set him on his own animal, brought him to an inn, and took care of him."

Luke 10: 30-34

There are three types of people in these verses. They are the thieves, those without compassion, and the one with compassion. In today's society we have those who unrighteously take, those who see a need and do nothing, and those who see a need and are moved into action by compassion. Be a person of compassion today.

☐ Pray   ☐ Read   Currently working on _____

Evening Reflection

Day 314

"However, the Most High does not dwell in temples made with hands, as the prophet says:"

Acts 7:48

The Lord lives in us. He does not live in any building. Why do we put so much into our places of worship these days? Is God able to accomplish more based on the quality of our facilities? Can the Lord accomplish more in our state of the art facilities than He can in buildings made of tin in Africa? Would you go to church if it didn't have heating or air conditioning? What about if you had to sit on the floor or swat the flies and mosquitoes away? Today, determine if you are more committed to Christ or to comfort.

☐ Pray   ☐ Read   Currently working on _____

Evening Reflection

Day 315

NeedToBreathe's song "Let Us Love" challenges us to love
others like we did when we were kids.

Go to www.StumblingServant.com and click on the Morning
Thoughts Song Challenges link, then Day 315. There you will
find a link where you can read the lyrics to this song while
listening to it. My nephew, Drake, has taught me so much
about love. He is so outgoing and hasn't learned any of our
world's biases yet. Today, love others like we did when we
were children--before we were hardened by this world.

☐ Pray   ☐ Read   Currently working on _____

Evening Reflection

Day 316

"But you shall receive power when the Holy Spirit has come upon you; and you shall be witnesses to Me in Jerusalem, and in all Judea and Samaria, and to the end of the earth."

Acts 1:8

Jesus was telling them they were to spread His love in their hometowns and to branch out with it all the way around the world. I think we do a pretty good job sending missionaries around the world, but I believe we fall short when it comes to our own hometowns. What are you doing in your community to show others the love of Christ? Inviting people to Church is a good thing, but Christ called us to minister to those neglected by others. I am a part of a group that formed The Barnabas Society, a 501(c)(3) nonprofit, non-government, Christian organization. In the Bible, Barnabas, was always encouraging people. Our goal is to unite believers in order to meet the needs of people by showing them the love of Christ. We must not think that our job is done because we are supporting missionaries around the world and inviting people to church. Find a need in your community, and ask others to help you meet it. Check out The Barnabas Society's website: www.TheBarnabasSociety.com

☐ Pray   ☐ Read   Currently working on _____

Evening Reflection

340

Day 317

"You also be patient. Establish your hearts, for the coming of the Lord is at hand."

James 5:8

"Be patient." That is easier to say than to do, but it is something we must learn. If we are set on doing things on our schedule, then we will end up getting ourselves into bad situations. As you have heard before, the Lord is never late, never early, but always right on time. Today, focus on doing your part, and patiently wait on the Lord to do His.

☐ Pray   ☐ Read   Currently working on _____

Evening Reflection

Day 318

"If your enemy is hungry, give him bread to eat; And if he is thirsty, give him water to drink;"

Proverbs 25:21

Say what? God really expects us to help out those who make fun of us, talk about us behind our back, spread rumors about us, and do other harmful things to us? He not only expects it, He commands us to do it. Do something today to show the love of Christ to someone that does not like you.

☐ Pray   ☐ Read   Currently working on _____

Evening Reflection

Day 319

"Do not overwork to be rich; Because of your own understanding, cease! Will you set your eyes on that which is not? For riches certainly make themselves wings; They fly away like an eagle toward heaven."

Proverbs 23:4-5

What are you focused on? That is more than likely what you spend most of your free time on. If you get that promotion, the company could close in the next year. If you buy that house, it could be destroyed in a fire or a storm. If you buy that car, it could be totaled or stolen. So many of the things we work so hard to attain can disappear in the blink of an eye. None of those things are wrong to get, but don't work so much to get them that your relationship with Christ or your family suffers. Take time today to make sure your priorities are in the correct order.

☐ Pray ☐ Read Currently working on _____

Evening Reflection

Day 320

"I marvel that you are turning away so soon from Him
who called you in the grace of Christ, to a different gospel,
which is not another; but there are some who trouble you
and want to pervert the gospel of Christ."

Galatians 1:6-7

If you give, God will give you a new car. If you are going
through trials, you aren't serving God. If you give more, God
will give you a new house. If you are sick, you don't have
enough faith to be healed. What would Christ say about these
things? What would Christ say about us allowing people to
scam others with these types of beliefs? Today, reflect on the
people in your life and see if any of them are being misled by
someone who is perverting the gospel of Christ.

☐ Pray   ☐ Read   Currently working on _____

Evening Reflection

344

Day 321

"And it happened when He was in a certain city, that behold, a man who was full of leprosy saw Jesus; and he fell on his face and implored Him, saying, Lord, if You are willing, You can make me clean."

Luke 5:12

I think if this verse were placed in our current context, it would sound more like, "And it happened when He was in a certain city, that behold, a man/woman who was full of (insert any disease you want) saw Jesus; and ran toward Him yelling, 'Lord, do you know who I am and all the things I have done for you? Why haven't you healed me yet? I have been praying for months and need you to heal me….'" There is a sense of entitlement in our country and churches today. God does not owe us anything. Today, start to live a life of appreciation, not entitlement.

☐ Pray   ☐ Read   Currently working on _____

Evening Reflection

Day 322

"For a righteous man may fall seven times And rise again,
But the wicked shall fall by calamity."

Proverbs 24:16

Have you fallen down? Not spiritually, but physically? Sure you have. At some point we have all fallen down. I can remember falling down quite a few times. Normally, it was while I was trying to show off. What would happen if we fell down and just stayed there? Most likely people would come over to see if we were ok. What would happen if we were still there an hour, a day, a week, a month, or a year later? It seems ridiculous that someone who is physically able to get up would just stay where they fell. So what about failing in other areas of our lives? We all fail. We all fail daily on some level. Maybe you fail a test, miss a game winning shot, don't have the courage to share your faith, fall apart during an interview, give in to your biggest temptation, or are disrespectful to your children. It's not about falling or not. It's about getting back up and how long it takes. You can't change the past. There are no delete buttons in life. We can either choose to allow our past failures to keep us down, or we can choose to learn from them and move forward. Choose to get up and move forward today.

☐ Pray   ☐ Read   Currently working on _____

Evening Reflection

Day 323

"Then Peter opened his mouth and said: 'In truth I perceive that God shows no partiality. But in every nation whoever fears Him and works righteousness is accepted by Him.'"

Acts 10:34-35

"In every nation." These are words we need to take to heart. God doesn't just accept people from a certain country. People are not rejected by God because they are born in a certain place. Why is it that we often choose who we share His love with based on where a person is from? Have you ever thought, "They won't listen to me because they believe something different in their country?" Don't be partial with God's love today just because someone is from a different place.

☐ Pray ☐ Read Currently working on _____

Evening Reflection

Day 324

"Do not be envious of evil men,
Nor desire to be with them."

Proverbs 24:1

Not only does this verse tell us not to be envious of people who do evil, but we are also told not to desire to be with them. It is easy to see someone doing wrong and think that you could pull it off too. Whether it is cheating on a test, selling drugs, having an affair, or cutting corners at work, don't do anything that will have a negative impact on your character today.

☐ Pray   ☐ Read   Currently working on _____

Evening Reflection

Day 325

"Every branch in Me that does not bear fruit He takes away; and every branch that bears fruit He prunes, that it may bear more fruit."

John 15:2

Do you pray for the Lord to take things out of your life that hinder you from becoming more like Him? Do you know things in your life that are stumbling blocks for you? I know I have some stumbling blocks. I also know that there are things that I don't even realize yet that need to be taken away. Evaluate your friendships, the things you watch, the things you listen to, the way you talk, the attitude you have toward others, the places you go, the things you do, and anything else that comes to mind. Determine if those things lead you closer to Christ, or if you are allowing them to keep you from Him. Would you rather be removed or pruned? Ask the Lord to start cutting away the things in your life that are not pleasing to Him.

☐ Pray ☐ Read Currently working on _____

Evening Reflection

Day 326

"For as the body is one and has many members, but all the members of that one body, being many, are one body, so also is Christ."

1 Corinthians 12:12

All those who have a personal relationship with Jesus are of the same body. Scott Anderson, a friend of mine, was born with cerebral palsy and has spent much of his life in a wheelchair, but he has not allowed that to stop him. He travels around the world speaking and telling others about the love of Christ. At a recent retreat, he was talking about the body of Christ, and he said, "I am sick and tired of the body of Christ looking like me." He talked about how we as Christians cripple the body of Christ. Why does it take some sort of major disaster for local churches who share the same beliefs to work together? Satan's attack on our communities is unified, but those who know the love of Christ refuse to work together. We are more concerned about members switching churches than we are about the youth we are losing to drugs and alcohol, the homeless who are hopeless, the elderly who have no one to visit them, the sick in the hospitals, and those locked up in jail. Today's challenge is to contact a fellow believer from a different church and come up with a plan to serve your community. Maybe it is just the two of you going to a nursing home, or maybe you organize a big event to help the homeless. It doesn't matter what it is, but today we must start tearing down the walls we have built that hinder the Body of Christ from serving as one. Check out Scott's website: www.ScottOnWheels.com

□ Pray   □ Read   Currently working on _____

Evening Reflection

Day 327

"Therefore let us pursue the things which make for peace
and the things by which one may edify another."

Romans 14:19

It seems to me that some people like peace while others like
conflict and drama. Is it possible to edify (build up) another
person while in some sort of conflict? Think of all the time
we spend arguing over meaningless things. Focus on building
someone up today rather than proving them wrong.

☐ Pray   ☐ Read   Currently working on _____

Evening Reflection

Day 328

"He who passes by and meddles in a quarrel not his own Is like one who takes a dog by the ears."

Proverbs 26:17

I have never grabbed a dog by its ears, but I am guessing by this verse it is something you don't want to do. Do you find it easy to join in when you hear people talking about someone else or something that does not involve you? No matter what you hear walking down the halls at school or in the break room at work, make up your mind now to avoid taking part in issues that do not involve you.

☐ Pray   ☐ Read   Currently working on _____

Evening Reflection

Day 329

"Then He said to them in His teaching, 'Beware of the scribes, who desire to go around in long robes, love greetings in the marketplaces, the best seats in the synagogues, and the best places at feasts, who devour widows' houses, and for a pretense make long prayers. These will receive greater condemnation.'"

Mark 12:38-40

Scribes were people of position back in Biblical times. What would you think about religious leaders of today who displayed the qualities listed in these verses? Any of us who display these qualities have no need claiming Christ, much less being considered a religious leader. It is my prayer that I never seek my own glory, and if I do, that I will lose any influence that I have. Today, pray the same for our Christian leaders and yourself as well.

☐ Pray ☐ Read Currently working on _____

Evening Reflection

Day 330

Toby Mac's song "Get Back Up" talks about not allowing
ourselves to stay down.

Go to www.StumblingServant.com and click on the Morning
Thoughts Song Challenges link, then Day 330. There you
will find links to read the lyrics to this song and to listen to
it. Today, choose to get back up.

☐ Pray   ☐ Read   Currently working on _____

Evening Reflection

Day 331

"saying, Go to this people and say: 'Hearing you will hear, and shall not understand; And seeing you will see, and not perceive; For the hearts of this people have grown dull. Their ears are hard of hearing, And their eyes they have closed, Lest they should see with their eyes and hear with their ears, Lest they should understand with their hearts and turn, So that I should heal them.'"

Acts 28:26-27

It seems to me that a lot of us as Christians need to take this verse to heart. It's almost as if we have put in the earplugs and put on the sunglasses so that we don't hear or see the needs of those around us. We have grown to believe that sitting in a building and listening to someone speak, singing in the choir, helping in one of the church programs, or speaking ourselves is all that we need to do. Those things are needed, but we are called to do more than go to church 1-3 hours per week. We are The Church, and we need to constantly evaluate the condition of our hearts. Tell the Lord you want to take out the earplugs and get rid of the sunglasses so that you can hear and see the people He brings you to help today.

☐ Pray   ☐ Read   Currently working on _____

Evening Reflection

Day 332

"You shall not go after other gods, the gods of the peoples who are all around you."

Deuteronomy 6:14

We have created a bunch of generic gods and claim they are all the same God, which is not true. The God of the Bible is not the same god that everyone worships. The God of the Bible sent His Son, Jesus, to earth to die for our sins. Jesus was born of a virgin, lived a sinless life, was crucified, and arose three days later to defeat death and offer everyone the opportunity to have a relationship with Him. Have you fallen into the trap that all gods are God? Are you worshipping the God of the Bible, or a god of another belief system? Determine today if you are worshipping the one true God.

☐ Pray ☐ Read Currently working on _____

Evening Reflection

Day 333

"He who despises his neighbor sins; But he who has mercy
on the poor, happy is he."

Proverbs 14:21

Do you have a neighbor you can't stand? Maybe it's the one
who gripes when a ball goes into their yard, the one who is
always having loud parties, or the one who lets their dog use
the bathroom in your yard. Do you think about how your
actions toward them reflect Christ and your testimony?
Have you ever taken the time to introduce yourself? Do they
even know you are a Christian? You can't control who your
neighbors are, but God can. Maybe He has put them there
so you can show them His love. Forget the things that have
happened in the past, and take time to try to make things
right or introduce yourself today.

☐ Pray   ☐ Read   Currently working on _____

Evening Reflection

Day 334

"Adulterers and adulteresses! Do you not know that friendship with the world is enmity with God? Whoever therefore wants to be a friend of the world makes himself an enemy of God."

James 4:4

"Wait a minute," you may be saying, "I've never had an affair!" Maybe you haven't cheated on your spouse, but you surely have cheated on your Lord. We all have. If we have a relationship with Christ and we return to the ways of the world, then we are cheating on Christ. We cannot live in the ways of the world and be living for Christ. Make certain today you aren't cheating on Christ.

☐ Pray   ☐ Read   Currently working on _____

Evening Reflection

Day 335

Monthly Prayer

What do you think about while on your way to church? What do you talk about? How long does it take you to get to your church? From now on, take just a few minutes and ask the Lord to be with all of those that will be sharing His word with others today. Don't just pray for your pastor or your church. Most of us have many churches in the city we live in that believe the same thing. It's time we realize that Jesus is bigger than the church we go to. Ask the Lord to give those speaking the words He wants them to say. Pray and ask the Lord to help you listen as He speaks. Ask the Lord to convict you and others of changes that need to be made. Pray that those who do not have a personal relationship with Him will recognize their need for Him.

☐ Pray   ☐ Read   Currently working on _____

Evening Reflection

Day 336

"Finally, my brethren, be strong in the Lord and in the power of His might. Put on the whole armor of God, that you may be able to stand against the wiles of the devil. For we do not wrestle against flesh and blood, but against principalities, against powers, against the rulers of the darkness of this age, against spiritual hosts of wickedness in the heavenly places. Therefore take up the whole armor of God, that you may be able to withstand in the evil day, and having done all, to stand..And take the helmet of salvation, and the sword of the Spirit, which is the word of God;"

Ephesians 6:10-13,17

Are you wearing the helmet of Salvation? If you have a personal relationship with Christ, then you have it on and it can't be taken off. If you don't have a personal relationship with Christ, then you might as well be in a warzone without a helmet. Going into battle without a sword would be like playing a football game without any offense. We must know the Word of God in order to have victory in our daily battles. How much scripture do you have memorized? Are you able to use the Word of God to defend yourself against temptation? Today, determine if you have ever started a relationship with Christ by accepting Him as your Savior. (Turn to page 11 to learn more about this) Also, identify an area you struggle with today and select a verse to memorize in order to help you overcome that temptation.

☐ Pray ☐ Read Currently working on _____

Evening Reflection

Day 337

"Now the LORD came and stood and called as at other times, 'Samuel! Samuel!' And Samuel answered, 'Speak, for Your servant hears.'"

1 Samuel 3:10

Sometimes I think we only pray part of what we should pray. What good does it do to ask God to speak to us if we aren't going to listen to Him? It's the same with other people. If we are preoccupied while someone is talking to us, odds are we won't really hear what they are saying. It seems that as a society, we are always preoccupied. How much of what the Lord tells us do we miss because we are too busy doing something else? Today, don't just pray for the Lord to speak to you, but also that you will hear Him as he speaks.

☐ Pray   ☐ Read   Currently working on _____

Evening Reflection

Day 338

"Be diligent to know the state of your flocks,
And attend to your herds;"

Proverbs 27:23

Are you a parent, a boss, a teacher, a brother, a coach, a youth worker, a sister, a member of a local church, a principal, a friend, an Aunt, a mayor, a co-worker, an uncle, a student, an employee, a grandparent, or anything else where you are involved with the same group of people on a regular basis? If so, you are a part of a flock. Many of us are a part of more than one flock or herd. Do you really care about those around you? Are you diligent to know how they are doing and what is going on in their lives? Do you try to find out if they have any needs you can attend to? Do you know where they will spend their eternity? I realize most Biblical scholars, of which I am not, would probably say this is out of context, but I think it applies. We all have influence in the different flocks we are a part of. Start to genuinely care for those around you today because you are a part of the flock of Christ, and that is what He would have us do.

☐ Pray   ☐ Read   Currently working on _____

Evening Reflection

Day 339

"'Is it time for you yourselves to dwell in your paneled houses, and this temple to lie in ruins?' Now therefore, thus says the LORD of hosts: 'Consider your ways!'"

Haggai 1:4-5

What percentage of places of worship do you think lie in ruins today? If my area is a representation of the entire country, I would say it is a very small percentage. If the Lord came and gave us a report on how we are doing things, do you think He would ask why our places of worship are so extravagant while our communities lie in ruins? Do you think He would ask us why we spend so much money on luxuries while missionaries around the world need funds to help those in true poverty? Evaluate your level of luxury today, and determine where you can make some cuts to support someone who has sacrificed comfort to serve the Lord.

☐ Pray   ☐ Read   Currently working on _____

Evening Reflection

Day 340

"A man's steps are of the LORD; How then can a man understand his own way?"

Proverbs 20:24

What's going on in your life? Are you seeking after Christ but can't seem to understand what is going on? Does it seem like doors are being shut that you thought He had opened? Have you been denied by the college you thought He was leading you to? Did you not get the job that seemed to be exactly what He had put on your heart? The bottom line is we aren't going to understand why everything happens. We can either choose to get discouraged or choose to believe that He has a plan. If you are seeking after Christ, then trust that His plan is better than yours, and don't try to understand it in its entirety today.

☐ Pray   ☐ Read   Currently working on _____

Evening Reflection

Day 341

"When a man's ways please the LORD, He makes even his enemies to be at peace with him."

Proverbs 16:7

Who doesn't desire this? If we desire something, we will work toward it. Today, choose to do things in ways that please the Lord.

☐ Pray   ☐ Read   Currently working on _____

Evening Reflection

Day 342

"The fruit of the righteous is a tree of life, And he who wins souls is wise."

Proverbs 11:30

Based on the number of souls you have influenced/are influencing for Christ, how wise are you? Have you had a part in someone putting their trust in Christ? Have you ever shared your faith with anyone? God has placed people in your life whose souls are hanging in the balance. Today, tell them about His love.

☐ Pray   ☐ Read   Currently working on _____

Evening Reflection

Day 343

"But if you love those who love you, what credit is that to you? For even sinners love those who love them. And if you do good to those who do good to you, what credit is that to you? For even sinners do the same. And if you lend to those from whom you hope to receive back, what credit is that to you? For even sinners lend to sinners to receive as much back. But love your enemies, do good, and lend, hoping for nothing in return; and your reward will be great, and you will be sons of the Most High. For He is kind to the unthankful and evil."

Luke 6:32-35

Knowing everyone would not accept Him and knowing those who did accept Him would not always be pleasing to Him, Christ still died for us. What good have you done for someone who did not know you? Have you shown the love of Christ to someone without a desire for anything in return? Today, think of something you can do for someone without them knowing you did it.

□ Pray   □ Read   Currently working on _____

Evening Reflection

Day 344

"Jesus answered and said to them, 'Those who are well have no need of a physician, but those who are sick. I have not come to call the righteous, but sinners, to repentance.'"

Luke 5:31-32

How often do you minister to "the sick?" In other words, how often do you serve outside of the church walls? There are kids in your class that need to see the love of Christ. There are people where you work that need to see the love of Christ. There are homeless people who need to see the love of Christ. There are sick people who need to see the love of Christ. There are abused people who need to see the love of Christ. There are incarcerated people who need to see the love of Christ. There are people all around us who need to see the love of Christ. Do you carry that love with you everywhere you go, or do you put it on when you get out of your car in the church parking lot? Do you desire to do more than sit in a pew or serve those inside of the church walls? Today, get out of your comfort zone and show someone the love of Christ.

☐ Pray   ☐ Read   Currently working on _____

Evening Reflection

Day 345

One of the verses in Francesca Battistelli's song "Beautiful Beautiful" talks about being able to see God in the midst of troubles.

Go to www.StumblingServant.com and click on the Morning Thoughts Song Challenges link, then Day 345. There you will find links to read the lyrics to this song, to listen to it, and to watch the songs music video. Today, evaluate your ability to see Christ through the troubles of life.

☐ Pray   ☐ Read   Currently working on _____

Evening Reflection

Day 346

"Look also at ships: although they are so large and are driven by fierce winds, they are turned by a very small rudder wherever the pilot desires. Even so the tongue is a little member and boasts great things. See how great a forest a little fire kindles!"

James 3:4-5

Have you ever looked at how small a rudder on a ship is compared to the ship? If not, try to find a picture. Have you ever heard someone yell, "Fire!" while someone replies, "Don't worry about it, it's just a little one." A "little" fire can devour acres of land in a matter of minutes. The things we say have the potential to do far more damage than we think. Make sure your words aren't starting any "little" fires today.

☐ Pray ☐ Read Currently working on _____

Evening Reflection

Day 347

"But avoid foolish disputes, genealogies, contentions,
and strivings about the law; for they are unprofitable
and useless."

Titus 3:9

How much more would we accomplish as Christians if we
quit our petty arguments? We are called to serve Christ and
other people, not to waste our time with useless debates. This
applies to other areas as well. In pre-marriage counseling, my
wife and I were told not to worry about being right. It seems
simple, but it can make a world of difference. It doesn't mean
you should change your views, but you also don't have to
defend your view by producing exhibits A-F on why someone
else is wrong. Today, don't waste your time trying to prove
someone else wrong over something that is useless.

☐ Pray   ☐ Read   Currently working on _____

Evening Reflection

Day 348

"If you faint in the day of adversity, Your strength is small."

Proverbs 24:10

There is no beating around the bush with this verse. A person's true strength is visible during times of adversity. It isn't so hard to be "strong" in your faith in daily life. The real challenge comes when everything comes crashing down around you. The difference in people who faint when adversity rears its head and those who stand strong in the face of adversity is preparation. Our spiritual strength is the same as our physical strength. If we don't put in work, we won't become stronger. Adversity is coming my way. It is coming your way as well. It's not a matter of if, but when. We don't know how big it will be or for how long it will last, but we know it is coming. Start your preparation today to stand strong through Christ in the face of adversity.

☐ Pray   ☐ Read   Currently working on _____

Evening Reflection

Day 349

"For riches are not forever, Nor does a crown endure
to all generations."

Proverbs 27:24

If crowns don't last, then what will? It's a shame that we put
so much stock into things that will fade away. Start working
today towards doing something that will have a positive
impact on others once you are gone.

☐ Pray   ☐ Read   Currently working on _____

Evening Reflection

Day 350

"Plans are established by counsel; By wise counsel wage war."

Proverbs 20:18

My philosophy is don't fight for anything you aren't willing to die for. I believe there are things worth waging war over, but I also believe the majority of us, myself included, would be more likely to react immediately rather than to seek counsel. When we think of war, we think of the battlefield. War does not always have to be a physical fight. It could be an emotional fight, a moral fight, an ethical fight, or something of that nature. Death can be more than physical death. It could be the loss of a job and relationships at work for standing against something your company does. It could be the loss of friends for not giving in to the temptations of this world. No matter what type of war you are in, or are thinking about beginning, make sure you have some wise people that can help you make it through. Don't do anything in haste today.

☐ Pray ☐ Read Currently working on _____

Evening Reflection

Day 351

"Therefore I say to you, do not worry about your life, what you will eat or what you will drink; nor about your body, what you will put on. Is not life more than food and the body more than clothing? Look at the birds of the air, for they neither sow nor reap nor gather into barns; yet your heavenly Father feeds them. Are you not of more value than they?"

Matthew 6:25-26

I'm not sure that many people in America, other than those who lived during the depression, really relate to these verses. Yes, there are those in our country today who do not know where their next meal will come from, but I would say the majority of us don't worry about that. Unless you have a health issue and missing a meal could harm you, I want to challenge you today. Don't take a lunch with you to school, work, or wherever you are going today. Don't bring any money with you to buy lunch, and don't ask anyone for food. Only accept food if it is offered to you. Today, try to understand what it is like to not know if you will eat the next meal or not.

☐ Pray ☐ Read Currently working on _____

Evening Reflection

Day 352

"The sacrifice of the wicked is an abomination to the
LORD, But the prayer of the upright is His delight."

Proverbs 15:8

We don't know the motivations of others, but the Lord
does. Have you ever given something or done something
so that others would see you doing it or to feel good about
yourself? I know I have. When we do that, whatever we give
(our sacrifice) does not please the Lord. Today, evaluate the
motivations behind the things you have offered to the Lord
recently.

☐ Pray   ☐ Read   Currently working on _____

Evening Reflection

Day 353

"Behold, I send you out as sheep in the midst of wolves,
Therefore be wise as serpents and harmless as doves."

Matthew 10:16

This verse tells us to be wise and harmless. When a snake comes into contact with a predator, its first reaction is probably to get ready to strike. That can also be our reaction when we come into contact with people who try to bring us down. Today, be careful to be peaceful and not lash out at anyone who may provoke you.

☐ Pray ☐ Read Currently working on _____

Evening Reflection

Day 354

"Blessed are you when men hate you, And when they exclude you, And revile you, and cast out your name as evil, For the Son of Man's sake. Rejoice in that day and leap for joy! For indeed your reward is great in heaven, For in like manner their fathers did to the prophets."

Luke 6:22-23

Have you ever been hated, excluded, or made fun of because of your faith in Christ? If not, then you may want to evaluate your life. We must care more about living for Christ than what others think about us. When we stand before the throne of God, we will not be able to blame anyone else for the things we did and did not do. Be willing to do what God wants you to do today, regardless of what others say.

☐ Pray   ☐ Read   Currently working on _____

Evening Reflection

Day 355

"But none of these things move me; nor do I count my life dear to myself, so that I may finish my race with joy, and the ministry which I received from the Lord Jesus, to testify to the gospel of the grace of God."

Acts 20:24

Are you living your life for yourself, or are you running the race God has set before you? He has given each of us unique talents and interests, but it is up to us to use them for Him. Run the race for Him today.

☐ Pray   ☐ Read   Currently working on _____

Evening Reflection

Day 356

"And Jesus increased in wisdom and stature,
and in favor with God and men."

Luke 2:52

When we think we are doing pretty well, this verse should bring us back to reality. The Savior of the world increased in wisdom. Strive to increase your wisdom today.

☐ Pray   ☐ Read   Currently working on _____

Evening Reflection

Day 357

"saying, 'These last men have worked only one hour, and you made them equal to us who have borne the burden and the heat of the day.' But he answered one of them and said, 'Friend, I am doing you no wrong. Did you not agree with me for a denarius? Take what is yours and go your way. I wish to give to this last man the same as to you.'"

Matthew 20:12-14

How would you feel if you had worked at a company for ten years, and when they hired a new person just out of college, they gave them the same pay as you? What about if someone starts work in November and then gets the same Christmas bonus everyone else gets? We often derive a sense of entitlement from doing the things we are supposed to do. God doesn't owe those who have faithfully served Him for half a century more than He owes a new believer. He doesn't owe us anything. Today, live as if you are indebted to Christ, because we are.

☐ Pray   ☐ Read   Currently working on _____

Evening Reflection

Day 358

"So they departed from the presence of the council,
rejoicing that they were counted worthy to suffer
shame for His name."

Acts 5:41

When was the last time that you were glad someone laughed
or made fun of the things that you believe? I guess the better
question is whether or not you have ever been mocked,
put down, or insulted for living your life for Christ? Today,
determine if you need to be more bold in the way you live
your life for Christ.

☐ Pray   ☐ Read   Currently working on _____

Evening Reflection

Day 359

"Enter by the narrow gate; for wide is the gate and broad is the way that leads to destruction, and there are many who go in by it. Because narrow is the gate and difficult is the way which leads to life, and there are few who find it."

Matthew 7:13-14

Which path are you on? If you aren't sure, then evaluate how many other people are living the way you are. If you are doing the things most of the people your age are doing, then you probably aren't on the narrow path since the verse says "few" find the narrow way. What would happen if you posted a video on the internet of you saying you were a Christian and that you were living your life for Christ to the best of your ability? Could you even do it? Do you have enough courage to do it? If your friends could comment on the video, what would they say? Would they laugh and ask what you were talking about? Would they mention what you did the weekend before? Figure out what path you are on today. If it is not the narrow path, pray and ask the Lord to bring you some people to help you get on the right path.

☐ Pray   ☐ Read   Currently working on _____

Evening Reflection

Day 360

Hillsong United's song "From the Inside Out" is probably my favorite worship song. If we want to make a difference on this earth we must give God control of our life and be totally consumed by Him.

Go to www.StumblingServant.com and click on the Morning Thoughts Song Challenges link, then Day 360. There you will find links to read the lyrics to this song, to listen to it, and to watch Hillsong United perform it. Strive to live out the message of this song each day for the rest of your life.

☐ Pray   ☐ Read   Currently working on _____

Evening Reflection

Day 361

"But they kept silent, for on the road they had disputed among themselves who would be the greatest. And He sat down, called the twelve, and said to them, 'If anyone desires to be first, he shall be last of all and servant of all.'"

Mark 9:34-35

If you want to be great, then serve. If you want to be a great employee, then serve. If you want to be a great teacher, then serve. If you want to be a great student, then serve. If you want to be a great boss, then serve. If you want to be a great husband, then serve. If you want to be a great wife, then serve. If you want to be a great parent, then serve. If you want to be a great child, then serve. If you want to be a great sibling, then serve. If you want to be a great friend, then serve. If you want to be a great role model, then serve. If you want to be a great team, then serve. If you want to be a great local church, then serve. If you want to be great today, then serve.

☐ Pray ☐ Read Currently working on _____

Evening Reflection

Day 362

"and for me, that utterance may be given to me, that I may open my mouth boldly to make known the mystery of the gospel, for which I am an ambassador in chains; that in it I may speak boldly, as I ought to speak."

Ephesians 6:19-20

One of dictionary.com's definitions of ambassador is "a diplomatic official of the highest rank, sent by one sovereign or state to another as its resident representative." Our sovereign Savior has called us to be a representative for Him while we are residents on Earth. He has called us to do it boldly. In order to be bold about something, you must believe it with everything you have and be committed 100%. If you are prepared to live boldly, then start today. If you need to work on believing with all that you have or on being committed, then make today the first day of your path to boldness.

☐ Pray   ☐ Read   Currently working on _____

Evening Reflection

Day 363

"Again, when a righteous man turns from his righteousness and commits iniquity, and I lay a stumbling block before him, he shall die; because you did not give him warning, he shall die in his sin, and his righteousness which he has done shall not be remembered; but his blood I will require at your hand."

Ezekiel 3:20

I'll never forget the first time I remember reading this verse. I was about to go to the track when our pastor called to tell my mom that a friend I had grown up with had overdosed on drugs and died. My mom wasn't home so he told me. I called my mom, but she didn't answer so I left a voicemail. After her voicemail greeting, it took me a little bit before I could talk. When she listened to it she didn't hear anything, so she hung up before I started talking. She thought I had just hung up. I went ahead and met my friends at the track, but I didn't run. I just sat in the stands and thought. I called a friend who had just left to go back to college and a few others to break the news to them. After leaving the track I went to a friend's house (who is now my wife), and it was there I read this verse. I wasn't looking for anything special and certainly wasn't looking for this. I just continued where I had already been reading. When I read it, I felt like I had been hit by a ton of bricks. I knew he had been struggling with drugs, but I never sat down to talk with him about it. Other friends had and he had people willing to help, but I never did it myself. I don't believe this was the plan God had for his life. I know I couldn't have said anything to change the outcome, but I believe God could have spoken through me and done so. Would it have changed anything? I can't say, but I believe it could have. Today, say the things you need to say.

☐ Pray   ☐ Read   Currently working on ＿＿＿＿＿＿＿

Evening Reflection

Day 364

"We love Him because He first loved us."

1 John 4:19

God loved us before we even knew anything about Him. I don't know what age we are as kids when we first love someone, but I know most of us have been loved by someone else long before we figure it out. For those who do not, or did not, have the most loving upbringing, remember that the God who created everything loved you before you were ever born, and He still loves you. Today, take a step and show the love of Christ to someone that may not expect it from you.

☐ Pray ☐ Read Currently working on _____

Evening Reflection

Day 365

"Jesus said to him, 'You shall love the LORD your God with all your heart, with all your soul, and with all your mind.' This is the first and great commandment. And the second is like it: 'You shall love your neighbor as yourself.'"

Matthew 22:37-39

It is my prayer that, if you made it this far in the book, you have made some progress in fulfilling both of these commandments. The journey is not over. From here on out, strive to live for God and to show others His love.

☐ Pray ☐ Read Currently working on _____

Evening Reflection

Songs Without Music

Back in high school I was in a youth group band. That is when I started writing. We were convinced we were going to tour the world. During that time we wrote some songs, but we never put music to them. The next few pages are parts of some of the songs without music that I wrote. I call them songs without music because it sounds more manly than calling them poems.

Neglected

Neglected at will
And Betrayed by the day
I often break Your heart
With the things that I say
You're pushed to the back
And only brought to the front
When I'm caught in a bind
Or there is something I want

Your love is amazing
And I don't understand
Why You forgive
With a look to Your hands

Time after time
My promises break
And some of my life
Has been lived as a fake
There are so many things
I have said I would do
But time after time
I disappoint You.

Your love is amazing
And I don't understand
Why You forgive
With a look to Your hands

Why You still Love me I do not know
But I'm glad You choose to love me so

You're rarely first on my list
When You're on it at all
But time after time
You're there when I fall
You reach out your hand
And pull me towards you
Then I turn my back
With the things that I do

I can't understand
But I know that it's true
Forgive me oh Lord
When I sin against You.

Like A Leaf

Like a leaf in the water
I will go where You direct
I will go without fear
Because I know You will protect

You're the Friend that I need
More than the money or the fame
You're the King of Kings
And Lord of Lords
That will forever reign
You died upon the Cross
And gave Your life for mine
Knowing that I understand
That all will work out fine

Like a leaf in the water
I will go where You direct
I will go without fear
Because I know You will protect

True Friend

The last few days are coming
And the end is drawing near
As God's children we should not be scared
But there is one thing to fear
Will any of the people we know
Die and go to Hell
And if they will what can we do
To stop them from going there

We can be a true friend
And tell them about Christ
Let them know He loves them
And that He died for their sins
We can pray that they will understand
And come to accept Him
We can be a true friend
A true friend, a true friend to them

Will someone that you know
Die in the night
Will they wake up
With the morning sunlight
Who do you know
That you need to go tell
Who do you know
That is headed to Hell

Be a true friend
And tell them about Christ
Let them know He loves them
And that He died for their sins
Pray that they will understand
And come to accept Him
Be a true friend
A true friend, a true friend to them

About the Author

I am a stumbling servant of my Savior, Jesus Christ. I am nothing without Him. I mess up daily.

I was born and raised in Southeast Texas. My parents are two of the biggest blessings I have ever had. They set great examples for my sister and I as we grew up. I graduated high school in 2001 and wasn't sure what I was going to do. I started at a community college, but wasn't ready to be serious about school yet. I took a year or two off and then moved away to continue my studies. I graduated in 2007 with undergraduate degrees in Psychology and Kinesiology. After that I moved back home and began working on my Masters of Education in Counseling and Development, which I finished in 2010. While working on my Masters, I helped start a 501(c)(3) non-profit, non-government, Christian organization called The Barnabas Society. I married the most amazing woman I could have ever hoped for shortly before graduating with my graduate degree. She supports me, inspires me, encourages me, and loves me. I have truly been blessed more than I deserve.

I have a personal relationship with Christ, but in the Christian book writing world, I would probably be considered an outsider. I have a degree in Psychology. I don't have any Biblical degrees. I haven't attended Seminary. I'm not the pastor of some mega church. I'm not even a pastor. I never even seriously thought about writing a book until last year. I have a lot of ideas, but I thought this was the most important one. If we want to love Christ and others as we should, then we must focus on our relationship with Him daily.

Visit my website at www.StumblingServant.com
Follow me on Twitter @JBrosky1
Instagram @StumblingServant
Facebook.com/StumblingServantPage

www.ingramcontent.com/pod-product-compliance
Lightning Source LLC
Chambersburg PA
CBHW030909090426
42737CB00007B/138